MOBILE LEARNING MINDSET

THE PRINCIPAL'S GUIDE TO IMPLEMENTATION

CARL HOOKER

International Society for Technology in Education
EUGENE, OREGON • ARLINGTON, VIRGINIA

Mobile Learning Mindset
The Principal's Guide to Implementation
Carl Hooker

Editor: *Paul Wurster*
Associate Editor: *Emily Reed*
Production Manager: *Christine Longmuir*
Copy Editor: *Kristin Landon*
Proofreader: *Ann Skaugset*
Cover Design: *Brianne Beigh*
Book Design and Production: *Kim McGovern*

Library of Congress Cataloging-in-Publication Data available.

First Edition
ISBN: 978-1-56484-374-6
Ebook version available

Printed in the United States of America

ISTE® is a registered trademark of the International Society for Technology in Education.

About ISTE

The International Society for Technology in Education (ISTE) is the premier nonprofit organization serving educators and education leaders committed to empowering connected learners in a connected world. ISTE serves more than 100,000 education stakeholders throughout the world.

ISTE's innovative offerings include the ISTE Conference & Expo, one of the biggest, most comprehensive ed tech events in the world—as well as the widely adopted ISTE Standards for learning, teaching and leading in the digital age and a robust suite of professional learning resources, including webinars, online courses, consulting services for schools and districts, books, and peer-reviewed journals and publications. Visit iste.org to learn more.

About the Author

Carl Hooker has been involved in education since graduating from the University of Texas in 1998. He has been in a variety of positions in both Austin Independent School District (ISD) and Eanes ISD, from first grade teacher to virtualization coordinator.

Hooker is director of innovation and digital learning in Eanes ISD. He is also the founder of the learning festival iPadpalooza (http://ipadpalooza.com). As director, he makes use of his background in both education and technology to bring a unique vision to the district and its programs. During his time in the position, the district has jumped into social media, adopted Google Apps for Education, and started to build a paperless environment with Google Docs. He helped spearhead the Learning and Engaging through Access and Personalization (LEAP) program, which put 1:1 iPads into the hands of all K–12 students at Eanes.

Since becoming an educator, Hooker has been a part of a strong educational shift with technology integration. From his start as a teacher to his current district technology leadership, he has always held one common belief—kids need to drive their own learning. He realizes the challenges in our current public educational institutions and meets them head on. His unique blend of educational background, technical expertise, and humor make him a successful driving force for this change. Hooker also works as a keynote speaker and consultant through his company HookerTech, LLC.

Contents

Contents

Preface

In January of 2010 Steve Jobs took the stage at a major Apple event to announce the creation of a device that was in between a laptop and a smartphone. When he announced the iPad, the reviews were mixed. Wasn't this something that had been tried before, even with Apple's MessagePad (http://en.wikipedia.org/wiki/MessagePad)? How was this going to work in mainstream society when it was bigger and bulkier than a phone and didn't have the keyboard of a laptop?

At the time of the announcement, I was a virtualization coordinator for the district. The technology director (my boss at the time) looked at me with wonder when I got excited over this announcement. I told him that this is going to change the face of education. In response he said, "I bet they don't sell even a million of them. It's like a crappy version of a laptop, only you can only do one thing at a time on it. It doesn't even have a USB port!"

In retrospect, I should have taken that bet, as Apple would go on to sell a million in preorder sales alone. Flash forward a few more months. On April 2nd, I was promoted to the role of director of instructional technology. The next day the first-generation iPad began to be sold in U.S. stores. I point this all out to say that even with all the prep work and sweat necessary for a successful device deployment, some synergy is also required.

As director of instructional technology, I was taking over a dying role of sorts. Many districts were cutting the position at that time in Texas, and some felt it was a "nice to have" more than "a need to have" position. Knowing that going in, I made it one of my personal missions to erase the thought in the minds of the purse-string holders that my position could ever been seen as obsolete. In fact, I set out to do the exact opposite: make them believe they couldn't function successfully without it.

A big part of any leadership position is assessing risks. With the announcement of the iPad, my mind immediately went to education. How could these devices help students personalize their own learning? How would they enhance kids' engagement and their learning experience? Are those gains in engagement and personalization enough to justify giving every student one of these devices?

These questions plus many others went through my mind and those of many of the leaders in my district in the months to come. Ultimately, we tried a small pilot of six iPads at the Westlake High School library to see what students and teachers thought. They were extremely well-received, but with a bond just failing in the fall of 2010, the hope of ever getting more of them into the hands of kids seemed hopeless.

Enter the second synergistic event. A group of leaders including myself made a trip to Cupertino, California, for an executive briefing on what Apple's thoughts were on iPads in education. Before lunch on the first day the Westlake High School principal leaned over and said to us, "We need one of these for every student." At that time, iPads were considered purely consumptive devices, a nice way to read a book or take notes but nothing in the way of creation. That trip to Apple's headquarters changed all of that for those in the room that were skeptical.

When we returned, we went on to expand the pilot to around 70 different users. From special education students to principals to high school AP teachers, we had as many key stakeholders as possible get their hands on these devices to put it through its paces. At this point the iPad2 had just launched and had a lot more functionality on the creation end than its predecessor, namely the addition of a camera.

The pilot would go on to expand into Westlake High School the following fall and eventually expand to all 8,000 K–12 Eanes ISD students by the spring of 2013. Here's an early blog post right after launch of the pilot on the Eanes WiFi site: http://tinyurl.com/oez2now. Along the way, I've seen the highs and lows of having a device for every student, especially one as nimble and easy-to-use as an iPad.

This book isn't so much about the device as it is all the things we learned along the way. There are examples and "tech tips" throughout the chapters to help a campus leader who is heading into a mobile device implementation. The book also offers some ideas for adjustment if you've already started one. Some of these are interactive and will actually encourage you to take out your own device (if you are reading it in paper form) and interact. While a few of the examples will be iPad-specific, I took care in making sure the tools and strategies for campus leaders can be used no matter what the device.

What I hope you gain from this book is a better understanding of what effect mobile devices have on your staff, your students, and your community. With a better understanding of mobile learning, the tools and activities throughout the book will help you with modeling, becoming a "flat leader," risk-taking, building a culture of creativity and shared ownership, and how to interact with all the major groups of a mobile device initiative.

This book is one of six books in a series, which are written with a focus on different key stakeholders when it comes to mobile learning. While each book stands on its own, I feel that having the set will give all parties involved a better understanding of each other and can help create some common language and goals to help our students with their learning. After all, we are now at least 15% of the way through the 21st century. It's about time we stopped talking about 21st-century learning and actually started doing something about it.

Good luck, and thank you for being a part of this mobile learning revolution!

—Carl Hooker

INTRODUCTION

C ampus administrators preparing to lead a mobile device initiative on a campus must wear many hats. Part of that role encompasses preparing and encouraging staff to take on the task of purposeful integration of technology in the classroom. Another part is modeling and setting the right amount of expectations for usage. In the community, you must be a cheerleader in support while also keeping an ear open for concerns. We will address these and many other issues that arise throughout this book. It's my hope that in reading this book, you will be armed with many different ideas and strategies to help you lead the way.

How to Use This Book

This book will serve as both a guide and a resource at times during various stages of your mobile learning initiative. The structure of the chapters in this book will mirror the structure of the other books in the series, though the content will differ.

The first chapter is all about the idea behind "flat leadership." Creating a web of communication among campus leaders not only strengthens your leadership team, but also provides you with ways to get multiple ideas and strategies for improvement. Being a flat leader spreads out the responsibility and ownership throughout your staff.

Chapter 2 is dedicated to things to avoid when running a mobile device initiative. It outlines the top 10 things *not* to do from the viewpoint of a campus leader. Every campus has its own set of problems, from staff who are negative and dysfunctional teams to vocal parents who have only a limited view of the initiative and students who are tempted to do inappropriate things with devices. Identifying (and avoiding) common pitfalls can go a long way toward making the initiative a success.

Chapter 3 is an interview with Derrick Brown, principal of the Young Men's Leadership Academy (YMLA) in San Antonio ISD in Texas. Derrick is an inspiring leader who uses many of the traits featured in this book. His charisma and love of his job and staff form the driving force behind a successful mobile initiative. His interview was also captured on video via Google Hangout and is available to view if you'd like to watch the unabridged version. Look for a link at the end of Chapter 3.

The middle chapters of this book delve deeply into strategies and examples of what campus leaders in mobile learning initiatives do well to succeed. Cultivating ownership is part of it, but hiring the right people and adjusting team dynamics can also greatly affect success.

Chapter 6 looks at what kinds of expectations you should set for your staff and students. These expectations are a key part of driving the change from traditional teaching to a more student-led approach, which becomes much more possible with mobile devices. Chapter 7 ties those expectations into a formal evaluation process—the things you should be looking for in your classrooms. It's much more than just a check box on a form that indicates that technology was used in the classroom.

In the penultimate chapter, we'll see how the role of the campus leader interacts with the other main players in a mobile learning initiative. It's one thing to have strong teaching staff, but how do you hire those people without working with the HR department? Also, it is important to help your teachers receive the proper amount of professional learning and support. Last but not least, parents and community can make a mobile learning initiative sink or swim based on their support or opposition. A campus leader needs to dedicate a large chunk of time to visiting, listening, supporting, and even training parents to make the initiative a success.

In the final chapter, we'll focus on the importance of reflection and sharing of ideas. Many have traveled the road to 1:1 or BYOD, and if everyone had shared their experiences, we would all have benefited even more from the collective wisdom. If we don't share what we have learned and reflect on the mistakes we have made, we could potentially be hurting other students even if they aren't in our district. No leader wants that on their conscience, so we'll review why reflection is important and explore ways to share your hopes and dreams with others.

"Easter Eggs"

According to Wikipedia, an Easter egg is "an inside joke, hidden message, or feature in an interactive work such as a computer program, video game, or DVD menu screen." Why can't we also have these in books? In this book, I've hidden several Easter eggs that you'll have to uncover and discover. I've buried some in words, others in images. How do you reveal them? If you are reading this book in its paper form, you'll need to download the Aurasma app (www.aurasma.com/#/whats-your-aura) and find the trigger images to unlock the Easter eggs. Find and follow the "MLM Lead" channel to make it all work. Instructions can be found here: http://mrhook.it/eggs. Happy hunting!

CHAPTER 1

BEING A "FLAT LEADER"

You hear this phrase a lot lately: "When it comes to leadership and running my organization, I want to be a 'flat leader.'" No, this isn't some sort of strange parallel universe run by people who look like Flat Stanley. This is a common belief in style of leadership that the old, "top-down" pyramid structure of traditional leadership needs to adapt.

Wikipedia defines a flat organization as one with "an organizational structure with few or no levels of middle management between staff and executives. The idea is that well-trained workers will be more productive when they are more directly involved in the decision making process, rather than closely supervised by many layers of management."

In some ways, schools and districts have been forced to resemble the model of a flat organization because of reduction in funding. While we in education have little to no middle management, we do have some support staff (assistant principals, instructional coaches, librarians, etc.) who support the teachers but have no direct authority over them. This means a couple of things could happen when you place a certain type of leader in a somewhat flat organization.

A tyrannical leader, or someone with a real god complex, can absolutely rule over a school because of its flatness and lack of political structure. I've worked in a school before where the principal told us at a staff meeting that if we didn't like her or our jobs she would help us get a job at 7-11 (adding insult to injury, there, implying we couldn't get our own job at 7-11). These types of leaders don't last very long, luckily (unless their test scores go up), and so we generally have someone between tyrannical and flat.

A flat leader enables others to take the leadership role at certain times. One company that prides itself on flat leadership is Google. There, the owners and CEOs commingle with the coders and the designers. In a *New York Times* article titled "How to Get a Job at Google" (http://tinyurl.com/otypeno), columnist Thomas Friedman questions senior vice president of people operations, Laszlo Bock, about what traits that company looks for in employees. Laszlo said the top two traits are leadership and a willingness to learn. He goes on to say that a good leader knows when to step up and take control and when to step back and allow others to take control (and, in turn, build capacity).

The trick in being a leader in a mobile device initiative is that you can be too controlling or too loose with your leadership style, and possibly lose focus on why you are doing the initiative in the first place.

Why is it important to share leadership in a mobile device initiative?

There will come a time in your initiative when as a campus administrator you are faced with some tough decisions. Maybe it's a parent who's irate about the fact that their child now has a mobile device for the first time, or it's an app or program that just doesn't seem to be working right. Regardless of the conflict or issue, you have to remember why you are doing all of this in the first place. I've seen cases where mobile device initiatives have either failed or succeeded simply because of the way a leader addressed conflicts or issues.

In many ways, the more people a principal has as a part of their leadership team, the better. With each member of the leadership team on the same page, when issues arise, anyone can handle it, not just the administrator with the reserved parking space. You have to think about what would happen if you were out sick or on vacation. If an issue arises and the leadership team is all speaking the same language, it doesn't matter who addresses the issue—the outcome will be the same.

Another big reason to have a shared leadership, or a "transformative" leadership team as we call it, is that more staff are likely to buy in and be a part of the initiative. Think about what happens when two parents aren't on the same page in a household. What do the kids do? I know that in our house, if we aren't constantly supporting each other and upholding each other's decisions, the kids will eventually go to each parent until they hear the answer they want. Staff, students, and parents are not much different when it comes to testing a leadership team.

If you have a strong team that meets and communicates regularly, it's like having a multi-headed principal. No matter what the issue or who's asking, the answer will be consistent and the same. Also, members of the team each have relationships with a variety of staff members, so when concerns arise, team members will communicate those concerns back to the core team.

Optimizing Team Dynamics

Anyone who has been a principal or leader of a group or team knows that dynamics of a group can change as personalities change. Being a flat leader sometimes requires shuffling teams up a bit across the district. Since you are trying to start a new initiative or make it better, that also means making sure that the teachers who are comfortable integrating technology aren't all on the same team. It's a lot easier for a group to accept something if someone in their group is already a believer.

Unless you are implementing a mobile device initiative campuswide, most projects will start with a pilot of some sort. When we started our 1:1 at the elementary level, we made the grade-level teams apply to see which wanted to start as a 1:1 team first. This helped get our initiative off the ground and ensured a level of success for two reasons. First, the team had complete owner-ship before the initiative even started, so there wasn't any "selling" of the idea to the team that started it out. Second, because part of the application process was a commitment to training, they inherently agreed to learn and grow via professional learning.

When you do have a dysfunctional team, the chance for success doing anything will be extremely limited. Keeping low expectations and looking at ways to "shake up" the negative dynamic is the ideal way to overcome a nega-tive team. In the end, you'll want to make sure every team has someone who's either on the leadership team or a voice for your initiative.

Hiring the Right Fit

Now that you've built your leadership team and started to re-arrange your group dynamics, you need to be keenly aware of those dynamics when hiring new staff. There is a misconception that younger staff or millennials will be able to integrate technology more easily than an experienced teacher will. Bear in mind that preservice university programs typically do not prepare teachers for schools that have a mobile device program. New teachers may be comfortable with technology, but don't overlook older teachers who may have experience with 1:1.

Some traits to look for when seeking new team members are self-motivation and a growth mindset. Look for teachers who are willing to learn and grow along with the program and who can verbalize the benefits of the purposeful use of technology in the classroom. You'll want team players who are willing to collaborate with colleagues and who do not teach in silos. Ultimately, you want teacher leaders who can create magic with learning in their classrooms.

Creating Avenues for Creativity

Most jobs in the world have some menial tasks that no one enjoys doing. When I spent a couple of years in the technology services department, it seemed that every time the phone rang, there was some sort of problem. No one called to tell us that the WiFi was running great. While I knew that our jobs were making a difference, it was not direct teaching, where you could see the change and growth of students.

In an environment where you have no means for growth or ways to explore your passions, work can become deflating. Teaching can be very rewarding, but at times it can be very stressful. Secretaries in the front office spend hours on the phone, coordinating and communicating with families and sick kids. Everyone on your campus has a job to do, and figuring out ways to ignite passion and allow staff to explore creative outlets can make the day-to-day grind not seem quite so painful.

Google was one of the first companies to create time during the week for passion projects. Their "20% time" was centered around the concept that part of your day or week as an employee was spent working on something you were passionate about. Some of Google's most creative ideas (like Gmail) were invented during this 20% time.

In education we don't have the luxury of dedicating 20% of our time to creating or working on passion projects, but as a leader, making sure there is opportunity for that is important. Not only does that give your staff an opportunity to think creatively, it also creates avenues of ideas to improve teaching and learning.

Web of Communication

Finally, to make all of this work, you need a strong web of communication (Figure 1.1). In a hierarchal leadership model, there is a funnel of communication that slows the higher up the chain you go. If you create a flat leadership model, empower your staff, and give them multiple avenues to connect and communicate, things can happen much faster. While some things do need approval from the boss, creating this web means that whenever issues arise, the group as a whole will hear about them. Also, whenever ideas happen, they have many ways of accelerating from idea to action.

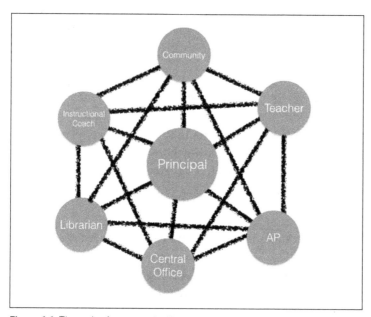

Figure 1.1 The web of communication.

The strength of this web depends on each of the nodes on it. Hiring the right staff, putting people in places that address their strengths, and building trust among the leaders in your staff make this web very strong. However, if there is a weak link, the web will weaken, and so will communication. With weak communication, it is harder to share ideas and get concerns addressed. Without strong communication, your initiative will begin to cripple.

As you embark on this initiative, think about your leaders and the web you have created within your school. You'll need strength in both to make this a success.

Sometimes, knowing what to avoid can be as useful as knowing what to do. In the next chapter, we explore the top 10 things not to do when launching a mobile device initiative at the campus level.

CHAPTER 2

TOP 10 THINGS *NOT* TO DO

Sometimes the best advice is to tell people what to avoid. Every district and school is different. There is different parent support, demographic makeup, teacher readiness, technology proficiency, and campus leadership expectations. This top 10 list should be a warning list for campus leaders who are either starting or currently implementing a mobile device initiative. Please know that this chapter could easily be 20 things, but these 10 items are the most crucial to avoid when embarking on this journey as a leader.

1. Do *Not* Forget to Set Expectations

It's amazing what a difference some minimal expectations have versus having none when it comes to staff using mobile devices for learning in their classrooms.

Let's make this analogous to what happens with students in a classroom and see how things turn out. In this first scenario, you give the students an important assignment that is completely different from any other assignment they have ever done. You tell them not only the expectations for completing the assignment but also that they may use each other, the internet, and yourself as a resource to support them. You also give them a list of expectations and timelines to complete it. Students struggle with this new type of assignment at first. They work together and share ideas on how to complete it. They ask you for clarification. They make mistakes, too—but in the end, they accomplish the task, even if they all went their own way to do it because you shared your expectations, offered support, and set timelines.

Now imagine you took those same students and told them you didn't really care when or if they completed the task. They still might have all the same support systems available to them, but without any expectations, only a few extremely self-motivated students actually finish the assignment. The rest continue working on what they've always been working on and what they are comfortable working on.

These scenarios aren't that far-fetched among staff, yet that's what we do with teachers all the time when it comes to goals and initiatives. You have to have at least some minimum expectations when it comes to the purposeful use of a device. It's a good idea to use something like the SAMR Swimming Pool model shown in Figure 2.1 (http://tinyurl.com/njwcv3d) as a way to get staff to identify one or two lessons they've done in the past that they want to take a little deeper with technology. SAMR is an acronym that stands for substitution, augmentation, modification, and redefinition. The SAMR ladder, which served as the inspiration for the SAMR swimming pool model, is a framework that teachers can use to assess and evaluate how students use technology in their learning. (To learn more about the SAMR ladder and how to use it, visit

Dr. Puentadura's blog at: http://hippasus.com/blog/). The SAMR swimming pool allows teachers to have some comfort in choice, but also sets some expectations that they must use new technology in their classrooms.

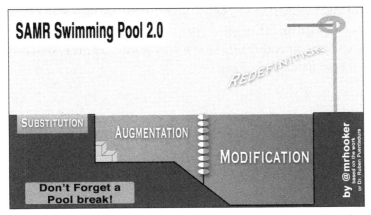

Figure 2.1 The SAMR swimming pool analogy was an idea that originated with Greg Garner's take on Dr. Rubin Puentedura's SAMR ladder.

2. Do *Not* Be Surprised by Resisters

Even staff that you have worked with for years and have built up great rapport with may see a change like a mobile device initiative as a challenge to their teaching style and pedagogical beliefs. The more successful the teacher, the harder they might be to change. After all, if they've been doing this teaching thing so well for so long, why should they change? While you might have the majority of your staff on board, you'll still want to work with those who don't see the value in the project by stressing to them that the goal is to improve student learning and success later in life. One value (I hope) that all your teachers share is that they want the best for their students. This can be a strong leverage point toward getting those resisters to change.

Parents will likely make up the largest group of resisters, depending on how supportive your community is and how well you communicate your expectations and goals for the initiative. Let's not forget that mobile devices are disruptive in both the classroom and the home—but unlike your teachers, parents rarely get any additional support to manage this change. Try to stay as open and proactive as possible when working with parents on their concerns. I think the parent support piece is such a huge part of making a mobile device initiative successful that I've dedicated a whole book in this collection just for parents. If they are on board and they get support from you and your staff, things will run much more smoothly for the students when they hear consistent expectations at both home and school.

3. Do *Not* Pass Parent Concerns to the Technology Department

It's tempting to blame the technology department for discipline or parent concerns. After all, the technology department is the one deploying this stuff, right? They are the ones who control the filters, so they should deal with the fallout. While this may seem like an easy way to "kick the can" on to someone else, the reality is that when leading a mobile device initiative, the campus leader has to own it.

When technology issues arise with student behavior (and believe me, they will), be mindful of a couple of things:

- The technology isn't going away, in fact in some ways we are becoming more dependent on it to teach and deliver curriculum.

- Often times the technology can catch or accentuate existing behaviors. Students will get on social media and interact. And while the technology makes it easier to access these "trouble areas" what we need to address is student behavior. If you've ever viewed the comments below some YouTube videos, you probably noticed that they were not written automatically.

Working with leadership to create a behavior plan and then clearly stating it to students will go a long way toward avoiding some of the classic pitfalls of gaming and inappropriate social media behavior. In addition, you'll want to have the students sign a form or oath of some sort that states they will use the technology appropriately. Figure 2.2 is an iPad oath that accompanies a post from the great Lisa Johnson (http://tinyurl.com/nnfund6). Lisa is an educational technologist at Eanes ISD and an international speaker on the use of mobile devices in learning. (Follow more of her work at https://techchef.com). Lisa does a great job of graphically organizing the rules and lays out the expectations (and consequences) for students.

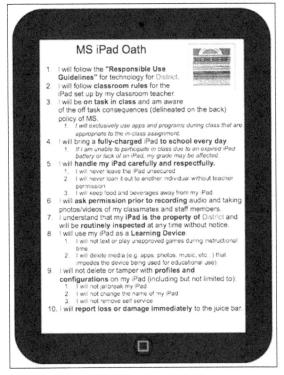

Figure 2.2 The MS iPad Oath covers the basics: ownership, time on-task, charging, app installation and removal, jailbreaking, and consent to routine inspection by the district.

4. Do *Not* Expect Strategy to Trump Culture

Ever see a coaching staff spend hours and hours on a new, innovative game plan? They show it to their players. They practice the plays. While the coaches are convinced their game plan will work, they never actually check with the players to see if they understand or even believe in the game plan. Then game day comes, and the players have to apply a plan they don't completely agree with or understand.

Guess what happens? They get blown out.

The coaches may have spent days and weeks on what they thought was the right strategy, but they failed to address the culture of the players and their willingness to accept the new plan. This type of situation I see repeated when districts roll out their new instructional initiative, grading policy, or mobile device plan.

Peter Drucker, renowned management consultant and educator, says, "Culture eats strategy for breakfast," and there is nothing like a fixed-mindset staff without any buy-in to sabotage a great strategy. When rolling out a device initiative, be sure to address the "why" and reasoning behind it with staff. Ideally, this is done with many staff even before the rollout happens. They need to be willing to accept and ultimately embrace the new plan or strategy long before day 1.

5. Do *Not* Leave All Professional Learning for the Summertime

How does farming affect professional development? Believe it or not, the industry that ruled American ways of life in the early 1900's set what has now been called summer vacation in schools. Intended to let kids go home and work through harvest, this phenomenon still affects the school calendar in 2015. With the exception of year-round schools, the majority of schools in America have 3 months off in the summer, and this is when professional learning for staff gets crammed in.

While districts do this for convenience, and it is better than doing nothing, in a mobile device initiative you will want to have opportunities for growth throughout the year. In our initiative we added professional positions, called educational technologists, at each campus to support the teachers and create just-in-time learning opportunities for staff. Not all schools will have funding available for that position, but with motivated teachers, you could find opportunities for staff to learn throughout the year. Bring in experts, pay for subs for site visits, or look for local conferences or "EdCamps" where staff can increase their capacity and continue to improve on their practice throughout the year rather than waiting until summer to learn something new.

6. Do *Not* Miss Opportunities for Staff to Visit Other 1:1's

Sometimes seeing is believing. Guy Kawasaki, author and keynote speaker on innovation and entrepreneurship, flips that a bit when he says, "Sometimes you need to believe to see." Regardless of which you believe, hearing scenarios and seeing videos of mobile device initiatives can help get a glimpse of the mobile learning classroom, but actually seeing it live and in action can be extremely powerful.

When we started a 1:1 program at our high school, we made connections with our middle school teachers and other campuses that were already in the middle of a 1:1 device initiative. We also took that opportunity to actually hold an "internal site visit" where our middle school teachers would get to observe our high school teachers in action. Anytime you can get an opportunity to have teacher leaders (especially the vocal ones) visit and see it in action, you will have a lot more support and traction with it.

7. Do *Not* Feel That You Are Alone

I think being the sole leader of a school can feel very isolating. But, it doesn't have to be. Whether it be with other leaders in your own district or reaching out to others on social media, don't feel as if you are in this all by yourself. Mobile device initiatives have been happening for more than 10 years in multiple states and countries, so there is a wealth of experience out there—you just have to find it.

In 2010, when we were having very early conversations about our 1:1 initiative, I reached out to leaders from schools in Brazil to Canada. The ability to connect quickly via a platform like Twitter or just by attending some national leadership events or technology conferences can allow you to build your PLN. For the past two years, we've hosted more than 100 leaders of mobile device initiatives at our "iLead Academy" prior to iPadpalooza (http://ipadpalooza. com). This academy encourages leaders to connect but also hear from industry experts and keynote speakers from all over the world. The bottom line is this: You are not on an island unless you choose to be.

8. Do *Not* Forget to Celebrate Successes Both Internally and Externally

Speaking of connectedness and social media—be sure to advertise and promote the wonderful things happening in your schools around your imitative. Eric Sheninger, former principal of New Medford High School and a thought leader on digital leadership says, "If you aren't telling your story, someone else will tell it for you." While it's important to share your successes and stories with the outside world, don't neglect to share them internally as well.

One of the best uses of faculty meeting time that I've seen recently is giving staff three to five minutes to do a mini tech talk on an app or project that they are doing in their classroom. While some staff can be nervous about presenting in front of their peers, eventually many can't wait for the opportunity to share the great things happening in their classroom. Presenting as a team can also be powerful to not only help those shy staff members but also promote teamwork and collaboration.

Sharing successes and reflections in a blog is one of the best ways to share things both internally and externally. Not only does it allow you a platform to share, but it also acts as a timeline of sorts for your initiative. Creating a blog around your initiative allows you to share the brand, the stories, the successes and the failures. We started with the WiFi Blog (http://eaneswifi.blogspot.com) and moved on to adding a whole section to our district site (http://eanesisd. net/leap).

9. Do *Not* Only Celebrate Successes —Be Open about Failures

As in a wedding, at some point during your device initiative you will make a mistake. Maybe the restrictions weren't loaded the right way. Maybe some of the paperwork wasn't ready. Or, maybe you short-counted the number of devices to hand out, as we did to our freshmen (I, of course, captured this on video for your viewing pleasure here: www.youtube.com/ watch?v=5-naWYMgJ28.

No matter how hard you try, there will be some mistakes. No one likes to fail, but I think the bigger failure is not learning from your mistakes. It's one thing to make a mistake, but we commit another if we fail to reflect and analyze what happened. This chapter of things not to do came out of multiple blog posts that I wrote following the first two years of our initiative. You can find those here:

- Top 10 Things *Not* to do in a 1:1 iPad Initiative: (http://mrhook.it/top10)

- 10 More Things *Not* to do in an iPad 1:1 Initiative: (http://mrhook.it/top20)

Again, I'm not proud of the mistakes that we made, but I do feel we owe it to the staff and communities that we serve to report what they were and how we addressed them. Otherwise, you risk losing trust within your community by painting a picture of your initiative through rose-colored glasses.

10. Do *Not* Force the Use of a Device, If It's Not Meaningful

A lot is written in this book about expectations, both the expectations of students and the expectations of staff. There will be an underlying pressure to have devices out at all times to prove their worth. Don't fall prey to enforcing that expectation, or you will pay the price later.

Staff that feel pressure to use devices in either a BYOD or 1:1 environment and aren't completely comfortable integrating them can resort to using devices as rewards during free time. When we did an initial walkthrough of our 1:1, we saw pockets of time in certain classrooms every day where 5 to 10 minutes of "free" time were allowed in classes. In a middle school day that has eight class periods, the amount of free non-instructional time really started to add up. In some cases, when you take class transitions into account and that free time, students were getting up to 3 hours of non-instructional screen time daily.

When setting expectations for staff and students around mobile devices, be sure that use of the devices is defined as meaningful use. In the end, it's actually better not to use the device than to use it inappropriately in class. Instead, work with your staff (and students) on coming up with alternate instructional uses for free time in class. Whether it be reflecting about learning on a blog or even reading an old schoolbook, learning can take place during non-instructional times of the day, too.

CHAPTER 3

INTERVIEW WITH PRINCIPAL DERRICK BROWN

What follows are excerpts from my interview with Derrick Brown, principal of Young Men's Leadership Academy (YMLA) in San Antonio Independent School District in Texas. I first met Derrick when he brought a group of teachers to our iLeap Academy at Eanes ISD. This 3-day academy brings in outside districts to both receive training from our staff but also to visit 1:1 classrooms in action. Derrick brought a team of teachers with him to participate in this event and to broaden their horizons with mobile learning. I could tell instantly that we not only had a connection but also that his staff truly loved and respected him as a leader.

A few months later, he returned with another group to be a part of iPad-palooza. This annual learning festival brings mobile learning enthusiasts from all over the world to celebrate the shift in learning brought about by mobile devices (visit http://iPadpalooza.com for more information). The theme in 2015 was "Keep iPads Weird," and Derrick *owned* it. On day 2, we had a "dress up weird" theme, and Derrick decided to bust out duct tape and LED bulbs. Even though he didn't win the big prize (it was based on crowd noise, and the crowd favored a donkey-kicking unicorn), his staff approached me the next day pleading for him to be a winner, too. It turned out that he'd spent several hours working on his outfit the night before, really modeling both the "maker" feel of the event and showing his staff how a little effort and passion can really lead you to all sorts of places. When his staff pleaded their case to me and shared his story, I was blown away. Add to that the fact that he had even given a testimonial for our iLeap Academy that day with a smile on his face—despite his disappointment with the costume contest—showed me he was not only passionate about education, but also extremely professional. All of this left a lasting impression on me. So much so that when time came to write this book on campus leadership, Derrick Brown's name was first on my list. Following is my interview with this inspiring school leader.

Derrick Brown

Carl Hooker (CH): Tell me your origin story. What led you from your beginning in education to now being a leader of this academy?

Derrick Brown (DB): Wow! That's a great question. I never actually wanted to be a principal, much less a teacher. Coming out of college, I started working for a corporation (a large insurance corporation). Doing that every day, even though I was good at it, was really, really boring. I started to look around at people doing that same job for 20 years and how depressing that was.

So I started looking around and saw in a magazine one day an advertisement for alternative certification for teaching. So I took classes through Region 20 [Note: Texas has many regional centers that support districts with professional development] to become a teacher. Began teaching in the Edgewood school district.

I remember my first day in the classroom when the kids were there. It felt right. I knew at that minute this is what I'm supposed to do. Everything felt good and right. I was drained at the end of the day, and it was so hard, but I just loved it.

You know, it's the kids. The opportunity to work with kids and their energy and their excitement. I simply loved it. That was fourth grade, and I did that for a few years, then I started doing music after school. My father is a musician, and in the summers, I would tour Italy with him and the band and ultimately do music with the kids. Every day was a way I related with the kids. I would always look for new ways to engage them by creating songs about what we were learning. They would want to stay to learn whatever new songs we made about what we were learning.

I also did a lot of video with them. You know, back in the day, we had those big old video cameras. We would make plays and film them from different angles, making props, learning about perspectives, etc. That took so long! But you know the kids would stay forever.

I remember the first Mac lab we got. I used to follow the tech guy around on campus and just learn from him on his break. When he left, I ended up taking over a lot of the things he did, so I was sort of the tech guy. A little while later, the music teacher opening came up, so I started doing that. I love music.

One of the things that really changed my concept of teaching is, I would watch all these great music teachers, but whenever I would try to apply what they did to my kids, it would never work. I remember a song that changed all of that. These kids wanted to sing a song for a talent contest, but I didn't know Spanish, so I was a little worried. They *begged* me to help them, so we ended up learning the chords and those kids learned to sing the song. They actually ended up going all over the city winning talent contests. That really showed me the power of what we are doing.

Are we just giving information or are we sparking an interest in kids?

Those boys, they kept playing and winning contests and that was really the first time I ditched the textbook and took a risk. I've stayed in touch with them since, and they are still playing music. One of them even has a record deal now, and I've gone to see their bands and it's still just amazing to me.

That changed everything. From that moment on, I wanted to include their interests in what they were learning. I ended up moving schools to teach drama and eventually got it to where the students were pretty much running everything. I treated them like professionals and made them audition in front of everyone. Kids would take that so seriously.

I remember a girl that would ask me in September what play we would be doing at Christmas, so I gave her a couple of options. I found out later, she got her mom to take her around so she could study for those parts. The day I announced the play, she said, "I want to try out for the lead part," and I told her, "We'll do that next week," and she said, "I'm ready right now." This girl did this on her own. That kind of initiative is what you want in kids.

She got the part, by the way.

CH: Wow!

DB: I knew after that experience, I wanted to take the things we did in drama and music and put them into a whole school. So, I started to get my master's and became an assistant principal.

One of the things I noticed is that change is hard in schools. Just as an assistant principal, I could watch and see little things and changes people could make in certain areas, but people didn't want to do it. Getting people to change their mindset and be open to the things I'm suggesting is a hard thing. Because I have all these great ideas in my mind, but not everyone is going to be as excited to change as I am. People will sometimes fight change tooth and nail. It doesn't matter if it's good or good for kids, they won't do it. My first instant was to fight that, which is actually a waste of energy, I learned.

Instead of trying mandates, I decided to open for people to try new ideas. I call it a "no fault zone." If it didn't, work I'm not going to try to hold you accountable for trying to learn something new. We'll learn from our mistakes and bring it back to the table.

It's not about me or my ideas, it's about innovation in a way that we are looking at what we are doing. It's about accepting ideas. Are we always looking for the best way to reach kids? It's about having a flexible and open mindset. I love learning new things. My favorite day of the week is Monday.

CH: [Laughs]

DB: That's the day I meet with teams, and we share ideas about tools we use and offer up ideas for better ways to engage kids. We started that here, and while it's only the fifth or sixth week of school, I've already started to see the change. I didn't mandate one thing. It's about them sharing or seeing what others are doing, then I like to go see it and record it to share with others. It's the freedom to do that and see what people are doing and sharing.

It's an environment built on constant improvement.

CH: How do you deal with a teacher that's reluctant to change?

DB: A lot of people will tell you to make it a mandate. I don't do that. You can't force people into liking what you like or wanting what you want. I expend my energy on great things. I don't spend my energy on things that are mediocre. So, if you're doing something that's mediocre, I'll meet with you and ask you if you'd like some ideas or suggestions to make it better.

What I've found is that synergy, when everything is rushing towards the "great train" as I call it, people want on board. Or, you get off. My role in this isn't to deter you, it's to support you in little ways.

I'm very high energy and I go very, very fast.

CH: Yes, you do. [Laughs]

DB: [Laughs] So, what I do is watch, and if you're not on the train, I'm not going to leave you behind. I give you a partner and something that you can manage. If you've never touched an iPad before, let me show you how to get your email on it and I'll send you something and you respond and we celebrate that. Yay! Alright!

We take it that slow. You can't be punitive just because you can't figure how to do this. We need to get them excited about this, but people aren't all going to be on the same level. We have to be patient. Rather than showing them how to do something, we need to talk to them about it and help them help themselves. It's about making people successful wherever they are.

CH: That's perfect. What about evaluating a teacher's use of technology in the classroom?

DB: Once again, there's that little box. You know that box you can check (about using technology). I've been in meetings where people have argued that touching the smart board is using technology or changing the light bulb on the overhead projector.

In my evaluation, it doesn't have to be about technology, but instead, what are you doing to engage? A lot of times it will get back to that, but if you're an awesome storyteller, then tell a great story about it. As I'm watching the students, I'm seeing if they are engaged with what you are doing. That doesn't necessarily mean that technology is involved, but it certainly does help with that.

CH: So where do you go for inspiration?

DB: I'll be honest. There are up and down times. If you are big in technology, there are times where nothing goes right. The lines are down and nothing is working and the passwords [are wrong] and it won't turn on. I get it.

Where I go for inspiration is always back to the kids. So, if everything is going wrong, what I've learned is to ask the kids, "What's another way we can do this?" I listen to kids, and they will tell me all kinds of things.

I've learned things from Twitter. I was never a big fan of Twitter, but it might have been in Austin at the iLeap Academy where I first started using it regularly. Once I got hooked, I was like, wow! This is awesome! These people talk about things that I was thinking. So, I'm following, and clicking, and linking—it's like a rabbit hole.

CH: It is.

DB: I like when I get an opportunity for hands-on learning or when people are actually showing what they actually use on a daily basis. That's the richest source for me for professional development. When people are trying to sell me something that they aren't passionate about and they might not even know how it works, it's a drain on my energy, time, and so I try to avoid it.

I believe in the grassroots. The other thing that has really changed for me is linking up with different people. I can go home and sit on the couch and pop on Twitter or search Google Groups and connect with folks. That's the power of that. I have folks that put me in their Australian group. I don't know why they did that, but they did.

CH: [Laughs]

DB: [Laughs] I didn't even realize they put me in their group, but now I'm connected with Australian teachers. That's the power of this.

CH: That's because there is going to be an iPadpalooza Australia, and you need to come now!

DB: Count me in!

CH: Ok, so I'm going to do some rapid fire. Are you ready? I'm going to ask you a quick question, and you just give me a one-word or sentence response.

DB: OK.

CH: What's a word or sound that you hate to hear?

DB: [Sighs loudly] … Did you hear it?

CH: That was it? The sigh?

DB: That's the sound of failure.

CH: Oh! I love it! What's something that gives you pride?

DB: My staff.

CH: Name something cool you have in your office.

DB: It's from *Star Wars*. It's Mace Windu.

CH: That is awesome!

DB: You know how I got it? We were buying a car for my wife and this was on the guy's desk and I said, "You give me that Mace Windu, and I'll sign the papers."

CH: [Laughs] I love it!

DB: [Laughs]

CH: Ok, so this kind of leads into the next question. If you could have dinner with any famous person in history, who would it be and why?

DB: Hmmm …

CH: Samuel L. Jackson?

DB: No, I feel like I already know him since I've seen just about every one of his movies. Let me think. It would be George Washington Carver. So many inventions, and you know what kind of passion do you have to have with a peanut? Every day, you know?

CH: [Laughs]

DB: At first glance, you are like, "This is a peanut," but then you look at the list of inventions, and it's incredible.

CH: OK, so along those lines here's my next question: What's something that needs to be invented?

DB: Along the lines of that group, we were just talking about (struggling teachers), I want to be able to do telekinesis. I want a telekinesis helmet.

CH: You could hold up an iPad and see what people are thinking!

DB: Yup!

CH: And move stuff! Here's the last one. Ok, this is pretty appropriate for you: What was the last time that you sang, and what was the song you were singing?

DB: Oh, man! I sing all day every day. I guess it was "This is YMLA." We won a video competition for PBIS and every day, now the boys on their own made it their school song. They want to sing it after the pledges. Every day they say, "Can we sing the song?" Now you're not going to get that they'll come up and start singing it to me, "This is YMLA, with character indeed." They want to sing that every day, and now it sticks in my head.

CH: I'm definitely going to put that video in the book! (www.youtube.com/watch?v=FuBR6EH6UOM) OK, any final advice for a principal about to embark on a mobile device initiative?

DB: Patience, my friend. Be patient, because some things are going to go wrong every day. Just celebrate what goes right.

CH: Awesome! Thank you Derrick Brown, principal of the YMLA, for joining us and sharing your stories of passion and leadership!

CHAPTER 4

BUILDING WITH THE END IN MIND

When you start a home improvement project, what do you usually do first? Do you go to the local hardware store and start buying random tools and supplies? Do you start randomly slapping pieces of wood and nails together? Of course not (although some of my personal home improvement projects may look like that).

You begin with a vision of what the end product will look like. From that idea, you build a plan. Part of that plan is researching what tools and strategies you'll need to use to do your project. Another part of that plan is estimating costs for materials and purchasing any extra tools you might need to complete the project. Before you start, you might also want to brush up on how to handle the tools and the best practices for using them effectively. After some research, purchasing materials, and reviewing the skills, you begin the project one step at a time in a logical order, so when it's finished, it will look like (or as close to) your original vision.

A home improvement project can be used as an analogy for your device initiative. We can draw parallels between them, such as the following steps we take to execute them:

- The Vision

- Research

- Tools and Materials

- Learning Necessary Skills

- Design and Building

- Evaluating the Final Product

Unlike home improvement projects, a mobile learning program has us working with people. People are far less rigid than a hammer, but it is possible for people to be as hardheaded! This, among many other factors, is why it is important to consider each step in the process. If we don't, sloppy workmanship will result in a sloppy outcome or could even result in total failure of the project. So, let's look at each step and analyze how you can use them to guide your campus initiative.

The Vision

When you set out to build your home project, you had an idea in your mind of what the project would look like. In fact, you could probably even visualize it. Sharing that vision with your spouse before starting the project would be a good way to avoid conflicts and differences in expectations (more on that in Chapters 5 and 6).

The situation is much the same way with a mobile device initiative. You and your team need to be able to visualize what you want a successful project to look like. Beginning with the end in mind, define the goals of what "success" looks like for your initiative. Gather feedback from a wide range of staff, community, and even students about what they define as a successful initiative. Knowing and communicating that end vision will help guide all the next steps of your initiative. Failure to do this "shared vision" exercise can cause many staff to feel disconnected and noncommittal about the project.

As a leader, much like a spouse in a home improvement project, you need to be comfortable altering your vision to meet the demands of others on your campus. If you want to roll out a 1:1 mobile device initiative or promote your shiny new bring-your-own-device (BYOD) policy, it would be wise to gather feedback from the staff. Sometimes having too many initiatives going at the same time can make the vision seem crowded. Failing to communicate the vision can make it appear blurry. Before you move further on, be sure the vision is shared—both in the sense that everyone feels ownership and in the sense that it has been communicated thoroughly.

Research

As I said in Chapter 2 (Ten Things *Not* to Do), you are *not* on an island when it comes to your initiative. Thanks to the magical "interwebs," you can now reach out to others for support. You can find research articles that support the ideas and vision you are trying to share with others. One person you'll come across quite a bit is Dr. Ruben Puentedura. As I mentioned in a previous chapter, Dr. Puentedura has accumulated three decade's worth of research about mobile devices and kids.

While his SAMR model defines quite specifically what tasks will be changed with technology in school, he also gives some great examples of what effective integration should look like. Much of his research can be useful when communicating with teachers and students on expectation of use. I was guilty early on in our own project of expecting all teachers to be completely transformative within a few short months. The principal of Westlake at the time, Linda Rawlings, reminded me to slow down and realize that changing pedagogy can take time, especially in a successful district.

Much of Ruben's research points out the same thing. Figure on a majority of staff spending the first 18 months or so working out ways to substitute and augment the technology before moving into the transformative deep end. Those who do cross over to a more student-centric transformative method of teaching and learning may still take three to five years to reach "Redefinition."

Having spent several weeks and months researching 1:1 initiatives, your vision and timeline for the project may start to shift based on expectations. Be sure to address whatever changes you make in terms of vision with your leadership team and how that might affect the final product.

Tools and Materials

All the research in the world is useless if you don't have the tools and means with which to apply it. Some of the skills will be discussed in the next section, but at some point you have to make sure you have the tools and materials required to make your vision successful.

If you buy a cordless drill that never turns on or work with nuts and bolts that don't fit, you'll fail even before you begin. Make sure that devices can access your network, that important instructional materials are available, and that you can transfer work digitally in an easy way. These are some of the basics in making sure your tools will work for your vision.

And while we sometimes tend to obsess over the device, don't neglect the thousands and in some cases millions of dollars that may have been spent on proprietary software that won't work on the device of your choosing.

Learning Necessary Skills

You've got this fancy new power drill, but how do you use it? Maybe you read the instructions or got a brief tutorial, but all of this really just scratches the surface of what this tool can do. After a few weeks of use, you discover from a neighbor that the drill can also shine your shoes and wash your car. Ok, so that might be a bit far-fetched, but you get the idea. Your knowledge level is important.

Handing devices to every student or allowing every student to bring their own can be a daunting concept for a teacher to comprehend. As I said in my top 10, visiting a 1:1 or BYOD district and seeing this in action is probably the most meaningful way to help teachers see the vision. After all, think about when you are doing home improvement projects. Generally, you search the web or Pinterest for ideas or projects that look like the one you want completed, right?

A mobile device initiative is much more than a 2D photo or even a video. It's a living, breathing thing that requires teachers to be adaptable with and develop growth mindsets. You can try to prepare them with some basic training or a device boot camp, but the reality is, until they see a mobile program in action or use it themselves, the learning will only be abstract.

One of my favorite activities is an interactive learning challenge called the APPmazing Race. This challenge takes the "learning by doing" approach and puts it into collaborative action. It allows the teachers to try—and fail—without being the experts in the room. Many who have completed the race have even implemented similar races in their classroom with students, thus modeling what they learned.

All of this is to say that there has to be some sort of training embedded in the process of building your final product. Some days might feel as if you are building the plane as you fly it, but putting those learned skills into action in the classroom will eventually help your campus reach your ultimate vision for mobile device success.

Design and Building

You've shared your vision, purchased materials, and learned the necessary skills to build your mobile device dream project. Now it's time to apply it all in an actual classroom setting.

One thing will immediately become apparent to a teacher in a mobile device-laden classroom: They are no longer the center of attention by default. The truth of the matter is, they may never have been, but instead of doodling on a piece of paper or staring out the window, students now have devices to occupy their attention. There are times when you will need your students' full attention. "Apple *up!*" is a familiar chant in our younger grades when teachers want students' attention. This has students turn their iPads face down, thereby putting the Apple logo on the back "up."

While some will go through classroom management struggles with the devices, the proactive teacher with the shared vision for the final outcome will start to deliver lessons in a more student-centric way. One of our environmental science teachers at the high school embraced this approach on day 1.

When visiting his classroom, you would see kids in groups of three or four. Some would have their devices out, others wouldn't. As I asked the students what they were all doing, I learned that each had a role to play in fixing a real-world environmental dilemma. Some of the students were rapidly searching websites on carbon emission guidelines, while another was composing a group email to a local congressman. This is a great, authentic learning project, but the thing that captivated me was that *none* of the students were off-task. They had their devices out more than in a traditional classroom, but they actually had less off-task behavior.

As teachers design their lessons and begin to build knowledge in their classrooms, they should be mindful of this approach and the impact it can have on learning. Each student has access to more information at their fingertips than any teacher ever could offer them. The role of teacher now becomes less of a "sage on the stage" or even "guide on the side." Their role now becomes more of a "mentor in the center" where students check in on various points of their projects, look for feedback, and ask advice.

One other bit of advice I'll offer is that the design and end product are often much improved if teachers consult with colleagues and peers. Too often, teaching is an event in isolation, yet many teachers share common subject areas and planning times. During the design and building phase of a mobile device initiative, you'll find that encouraging collaboration among a grade-level or subject-area team can only make the ending vision that much better. Just as you wouldn't bring in one person to build a house, teachers can all call on their strengths as a team to design these student-centric, transformative lessons and learning environments.

Evaluating the Final Project

Compared to a home improvement project, judging the success of a mobile device initiative is a lot less cut and dried. Most of that success is defined by your initial vision of what the result would look like. If it was just "All kids will use their devices" then you can check this one off your to-do list. However, if it's more in-depth, such as "Students will use technology to help address future-ready skills like creativity and collaboration while reflecting on their own learning," this can be bit more of a challenge to evaluate.

To evaluate a mobile device initiative, you have to ask the following questions when you walk into a classroom:

1. Are the students engaged in what they are learning?

2. Do the students understand the learning objectives of what they are doing?

3. How does the teacher know when the students have learned the objective?

4. How is the teacher differentiating for students who are struggling or excelling?

5. Who is doing most of the "work" in the classroom, the teacher or the students?

6. What role does technology play in helping with these questions?

7. If technology is being used, to what level or extent? Is it purposeful? How would you rate it on the SAMR scale?

When you look back at the answers to these questions, you will be able to see and evaluate the success of your initiative. You'll notice that the first five questions really have little to do with technology. There is a purpose behind this. Because our main objective and our vision of a successful initiative is effective and meaningful learning, our evaluating questions should reflect that first.

A common mistake in technology initiatives is to monitor the *quantity* of use versus the *quality* of use. You end up with many "flash and dash" type lessons that use technology in a sparkly way, but really have no meat or substance to the learning. An approach with more impact is leveraging technology to really delve into actual student learning. Having engaged students is the first part of that, but also creating avenues for students to explore their passions, apply real-world strategies, and reflect on their learning is really the way to make the use of mobile devices most effective.

In the end, when you look at your final project, you may see some imperfections, such as forgetting to send out a student device contract or another oversight. Ultimately, if you follow the steps outlined earlier and keep your end vision in mind, the initiative will be a success—and, much as in home improvement, you'll continue to work, build, design, and improve on it for years to come.

CHAPTER 5

IDENTIFYING STAKEHOLDERS AND CULTIVATING OWNERSHIP

Have you ever had a really good idea, but found that your friends were not on board? Early in my teaching career, this thing called the internet was really starting to take off. My wife and I were invited to hear a product pitch for something called "Peapod." The founders of this web application said it would completely replace grocery stores in 10 to 15 years. The concept was simple: You would type a list of grocery items into a web form, and this company would send you food from their warehouse. With just the click of some buttons, you could have food delivered to your door. So, shoppers would no longer have to navigate tight aisles with a shopping cart?

Sign me up! I was so excited about the idea that I even contemplated taking a portion of my $26,000 yearly teacher salary to invest in it.

Then my wife pulled me aside and started asking questions. She wasn't being negative, but she was also skeptical of this concept. What about people without internet? Where is the food coming from? Who's checking the quality of vegetables and fruit? What if they are out of what I want? You get the idea.

Although automating grocery buying appeared to be a way technology could simplify the shopping experience, it came with many issues. In addition to getting my wife's input, I decided to bounce the idea off my friends. They were all *completely* opposed to it. At that point, I started to really question my rationale and excitement for the product. If the people I trust and love have some real problems with the idea, I should respect and listen to their input. Turns out, my wife and friends were partially right and partially wrong. The concept of outsourcing grocery shopping would eventually catch on (more than 15 years later) with the advent of "Instacart" (www.instacart.com), but they were correct in telling me that this wasn't a wise investment at the time.

They would have supported me even if I had chosen not to listen, but this could have damaged some of our mutual respect and trust if I didn't express to them that I value their opinions by offering a solid counterargument aside from "I think this is a swell idea."

While this is a personal example, school leaders should use the same philosophy when gathering input for a device initiative. Your grand idea may not be so grand when people who will be directly affected have some say or input. As a leader of a campus, you have the most influence on whether a mobile learning environment can really be successful. Part of your influence is making wise decisions while gathering the input of others. And this doesn't just mean other campus administrators.

Variety Is the Spice of Life (and So Is Decision Making)

In the summer of 2015, my school board and superintendent tasked me with the challenge of finding ways to gather as much input on our mobile device initiative as possible from all concerned parties (students, teachers, and parents). While the name started out as a "Technology Task Force" (www.eanesisd.net/taskforce/ttf), I knew it had to be about more than just technology. Sure, we had $5 million to spend on our "Student Mobile Device Initiative," but that investment in hardware represented something much bigger than just devices. I asked that the task force be renamed "Digital Learning Task Force" to show that learning was really the point.

When the time came to pick people for the task force, the temptation may have been to load it up with other like-minded gearheads, but in reality, they were already on board with the philosophy of digital tools in the hands of every student. We ended up having an open application online that invited parents and members of the community to be a part of this next decision. More than 60 community members expressed an interest in filling one of the four to six spots we held for them on the task force.

In the end, rather than just simply taking the biggest tech advocates, we broke the groups into four sections (community member without kids, secondary school parent, elementary school parent, and a "mix/all level" parent who had kids at each level.) We had everyone from soccer moms to business startup dads apply, as well as teachers and students (even though the application wasn't for them). After making our selection based on their own input and beliefs, we set out to seek nominations from campuses for a variety of teachers, too.

Involving Teacher Leaders

Again, we could have made a "lay-up" decision here and just picked the vanguard technology teachers for the task force, but we needed a wide variety of representation from all subject areas and more. Picking the right teacher is more than just picking someone with technology prowess. They must have both of the following traits: openness to trying something new, and being seen as vocal and respected leaders on their campus.

Teachers are the ultimate gatekeepers of technology use in the classroom. Even a year after our initial pilot, we had reluctant teachers or those who didn't see the value in mobile devices. Some even told students to just put the devices away. Using the well-researched "innovator's bell curve" from the 1960s (which has been updated a bit to the Technology Adoption Curve seen in Figure 5.1), you can see that there is a "chasm" of sorts that you need to cross among the early adopters to make it successful. Once the early majority is on board, the wave of change will overpower those in the late majority and even some of the laggards who may never see value in the devices. Laggards hold this belief for a variety of reasons—fear, hesitation, doubt that the technology will work, or just that they feel their methods are already "successful," so why change now?

Despite those two extremes, you still have approximately 70% of teachers stuck in the middle trying to figure out which way to sway (resulting in the classic bell curve).

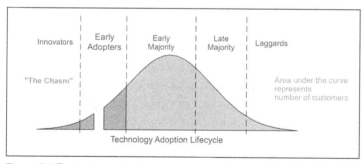

Figure 5.1 Technology adoption curve.

How Will This Solve a Problem for Teachers?

The middle group in Figure 5.1 represents the majority of staff. Depending on the experience and mindset of your staff, you will have a little more than 70% who are basically going to continue on their same path unless they see a convincing argument for how having mobile devices will help solve a problem for them. They aren't necessarily against having technology in their class (see the "Laggards"), but they may need some explanation or motivation to use technology that could disrupt their teaching routine.

This group is the most important to get on board because, as you can tell by the curve, once you've got both the early and late majority on board, the wave has crested and the laggards will almost be forced to join. So, how do you go about showing that a mobile device initiative solves a problem for those teachers? You keep it simple.

When meeting with teachers in teams or as an entire staff, be sure to stress that there are many different ways to integrate technology in the class-room. From organization to formative assessment, showing them a couple of different tools will help with this. Then set some minimum expectations that both "raise the game" of the teacher but also give them some relief. One effective way I've seen this done is telling staff that they should pick "just one or two" tools to add to their arsenal for the year, and when they have mastered those, they can add more. When you tell teachers this, it lessens the impact and feeling of "Oh my God, they want to force me to do what?" and instead turns their response to "Well, I can manage to change or learn one or two things this year."

Truth be told, teachers can and usually will add more than a couple of tools to their toolkit of technology integration, but just those initial baby steps and expectations allows them the autonomy of not changing everything they are doing. Once the students start seeing these changes, the buzz will spread throughout the building, and in a way, their excitement will get other teachers on board.

I remember a specific example in our 2014–15 school year at the middle school when teachers were introduced to the formative assessment tool called Kahoot! (www.getkahoot.com). Once a couple of teachers started using this fun, engaging tool to access student understanding, the students started talking about it. Within just a few short weeks, multiple teachers were using it, and by the end of the school year, when students were asked at a student panel, "Which app do your teachers use the most?" they reported that Kahoot! had taken over the classrooms at that middle school.

The ease of use of that particular platform, the educational value of the formative assessment feedback, and the expectation to use one or two different tools with the mobile devices made this a great first step in traveling down the road from enhancement to transformation as it's defined in the SAMR model (http://mrhook.it/road). Most importantly, it showed that the technology would not be an obstacle, but rather solve a problem for those teachers in the "majority" range of the innovator's bell curve.

Allow Multiple Opportunities and Avenues to Provide Feedback

Having an open-door policy as a campus leader is considered a classic first step in gathering feedback, hearing concerns, and addressing problems. As a proactive leader in a mobile device initiative, you shouldn't wait for the problems to come to your office. You need to be visible and available throughout the building.

While my current position is that of a district leader, I can almost sense that disconnection when it starts to happen. I'll visit a campus and usually hear things like "Wow! Haven't seen you in a long time." or "Uh oh, what's wrong?" meaning that I'm never present unless there is an issue. As a principal, you should never have to experience those two questions, but I've worked for a few principals who seemed to be almost unapproachable despite having their door open.

Getting negative feedback may not seem positive, unless you look at it as a means of growth and adjustment. Not getting feedback is actually more of a negative. As a leader, providing multiple opportunities and avenues for your staff, students, and parents to give you feedback will help better shape your program and address any concerns before they become larger problems. Not only should you provide the opportunities for feedback, but you should also encourage and promote it. The following are few ideas/examples of ways to generate good feedback (which in turn promotes buy-in):

Student Focus Groups

Listening to students' opinions can be amazingly refreshing and brutally honest. As I mentioned a few paragraphs before this, the student panel (Figure 5.2) is where we learned that Kahoot! had caught fire with teachers, but it's also where we learned that non-instructional apps were running amuck. Students shared their frustration with other students playing games and being distracted throughout the school day, which caused us to respond immediately with a "No Non-Instructional App" policy. Our campus educational technologist, Kacy Mitchell (@spearheadedtech), reflected on a recent student panel here on her blog: http://mrhook.it/stupanel. It's incredible to listen to the unfiltered voices of students when shaping your mobile initiative, especially when you consider that they are your "customers."

Figure 5.2 Our student panels are a great source of brutally honest feedback.

Teacher Focus Groups

Much like students, teachers are affected daily by the technical, instructional, and pedagogical challenges of implementing mobile devices in the classroom. As I mentioned earlier in this chapter, they need to be a part of every step in the process, and this includes giving them an opportunity to provide feedback in a safe, non-threatening environment. The teacher panels we've had in the past have revealed issues that we weren't aware of (such as Google Drive suddenly not working), and they made us aware of many innovative ways teachers have worked around technical issues and went on to do amazing things in their classrooms.

Parent Focus Groups

Having a community that supports your initiative can be the key to making it transformative. Whether the devices go home or you allow them into your school, parent support and feedback will help bridge the transition time between home and school. Hearing the concerns of parents and supporting them through parent workshops, meetings, and discussions will also help bridge that gap. Parents do lead busy lives, so getting a panel for a focus group can be a tricky proposition. One idea that I've attempted is having "virtual office hours" and hosting a Google Hangout where multiple parents can get online to discuss their concerns as well as their stories of success when integrating mobile devices into their homes.

Surveys

Tried and true methods like surveys can allow you to quickly grab a snapshot of the feedback from all of your user groups. Following are a few things to keep in mind when creating your survey.

- Keep it short and simple (no more than 10 questions).

- Try to limit the number of "ranking" type responses (i.e., "Rank the ways your mobile device is being used from least to greatest").

- The Likert scale can be a powerful way to gather quick feedback, but make sure it's more than just a 1 to 3 scale (1 to 5 or 1 to 10 can give more accurate feedback).

- Provide an opportunity for "other comments" or space where your survey takers can voice their discoveries and concerns.

To cultivate leadership and ownership, have members of each group come up with questions for their group. That helps in two ways: (1) It makes the questions more relevant and (2) it makes the survey-taker value the survey a little more because it's not just going to end up in some administrative folder somewhere.

Create a Hashtag

One of the more recent ideas I've seen used with social media is creating a hashtag around your initiative or program. Doing this instead of a user account means that no one "owns" the hashtag and anyone can comment or post a question. We did this with our Eanes Digital Learning Task Force (#EanesDLTF, http://mrhook.it/hashtag) as a way to crowd source questions and resources.

Create an Online Community

Another recent idea made available because of the internet and social media is the hosting of an online community site where teachers, parents, and students can post questions or resources. I've seen this done with Facebook groups, but since some people don't feel comfortable sharing their Facebook account, you could use a Google Community, as we did with the Digital Learning Task Force (http://tiny.cc/EanesDLTF). This allows for asynchronous feedback, and it is a great way to get more response from the shy parent or student who doesn't like to speak up at forums or focus groups.

Focus on the Learning and the Students

Throughout the process of cultivating shared ownership, there will be times when the device will become the focus. While the device is a major part of the learning and teaching taking place in your building, remember that the users are still the focus of this initiative. No device magically helps a student learn or purposely steers them to an inappropriate website or app. No device can supply a teacher with instant student feedback without the student interacting with it in some fashion, and no device forces kids to get on social media and become cyberbullies. It's all about how the device is being used.

I mentioned earlier that the student panel revealed that quite a few "non-instructional" apps were being used throughout the school day, and in fact this was encouraged by teachers whenever there was a "free five minutes" at the end of class. As a campus leader, the temptation is to block or restrict every game or "non-approved" app on the device in question. In fact, many districts decide on a particular device because it can offer a strict level of control. However, how are students learning self-discipline and discovery in these districts?

We have restrictions on our devices that keep age-inappropriate apps from being loaded, but this doesn't block broad categories such as "games" from being put on the devices. We have always had the option of pre-loading the devices with some set apps that only we approve and move forward from there, but that comes at a price.

Take, for example, a recent middle school student panel we hosted with some visitors during our iLeap Academy (http://iLeapAcademy.com). One of the eighth grade students revealed that he had been using a programming app to code and create his own apps. The app he mentioned appears nowhere on our list of "educationally approved" apps, but it does provide the opportunity to think critically. If we had restricted the apps, he would have never had the opportunity to explore or discover this app, and we would likely have never learned of its existence.

Besides gaming, bullying on social media or via messages can also shift the focus from the user to the device. Disenchanted parents will often point to the device as the culprit when such situations arise. "If only you hadn't given my child that device, this would have never happened" or "If my student didn't have to use their phone for learning, this wouldn't have happened." These comments are common, and it's easy to understand where they come from. In this new, digitally rich world where our kids can become "insta-famous" just by posting a video or clever meme, you can see a scenario where our lives would be easier as parents if we didn't have to deal with technology. Some adults also feel inadequate when it comes to their own experience with or knowledge of how to use a device, which can be both intimidating and frustrating for them.

One of the most important jobs for principals of a mobile device initiative is to both be a cheerleader and a listener to concerns and problems. However, by cultivating leadership and ownership throughout the school and community, those concerns can be handled by multiple staff, and the cheering can then come from all directions.

CHAPTER 6

MODELING AND SETTING EXPECTATIONS

P art of being a parent means letting your kids fail so they can learn to recover. It's one of the hardest things to do, because you don't want them to make mistakes or feel the pain of those mistakes. As both a teacher and a parent, I struggled with this because I wanted to protect my kids and my students from failure.

The truth is, in doing so I was depriving them of learning in some ways. A big part of the learning process is that experience of recovery and failure. But as the leader of the family or the classroom, I wanted to be seen as the one who knew everything. I thought that making mistakes meant I was less of a leader and they would have less respect for me.

One thing I've learned in my progression from classroom teacher to district administrator is that as responsibilities grow, the fear of failure increases, and the ability to serve as a risk-taking role model gets harder and harder. The more responsibility, the more ego. The bigger your ego, the less likely you are to be willing to take a risk. Teachers can also feel this.

Campus principals set the tone for the rest of the staff. If you are guarded and risk-adverse, your staff will follow suit. In a normal, traditional school, this wouldn't be an issue. Teachers can continue to carry on with stale, hand-delivered content because the principal doesn't feel the need to change—and the teachers actually fear change. This is especially true in schools that have had high AP test scores or excellent accountability ratings. While those ratings only account for one part of the overall outcome for students and schools, leaders are beholden to test scores and ratings.

Throw mobile devices into the mix, and suddenly students who were successful at winning the "game of school" become almost annoyed at the distributive change that mobile devices can potentially bring to students who have struggled with traditional learning environments. Suddenly the playing field is a little more level. However, the potential for not only leveling the academic field but also the overall well-roundedness of a student falls on the teachers (and the parents somewhat). Using mobile devices to personalize learning patterns, teach digital citizenship skills and responsibilities, learn "soft skills," and dig deeper into subjects becomes much more possible with the ubiquitous access provided by mobile devices.

Fiction writer H. P. Lovecraft once said, "The oldest and strongest emotion of mankind is fear, and the oldest and strongest kind of fear is fear of the unknown" (1927, p. 23). This is especially true of a campus leader. While reading a book like this one can help alleviate some of that fear, there is always some level of doubt or skepticism when placing devices in the hands of every student. That skepticism and doubt can actually be a healthy thing, as long as it doesn't cripple progress.

Administrative Modeling on the SAMR Scale

One of the great things about technology, especially mobile technology, is how new it all is. While some may say that's also what makes it terrible, in some ways its newness gives everyone a chance to learn things together. A principal heading into this initiative needs to walk the walk as much as possible.

That means showing up at faculty meetings, team meetings, parent discussions, and district committees with the device at all times. You might start out using it only to have your email quickly accessible, but before you know it, you, too, will start discovering different uses for it. I've often enjoyed visiting campuses where the principal was leading a staff meeting with an iPad in hand, even if just to look at some notes. Seeing that same administrator do walk-throughs of the classroom with device in hand modeled usage not only for teachers but also for students. "Hey, he's using the same device I'm using!" the students would exclaim.

Just as you would expect teachers and students to use technology in a variety of ways, you should also model some of that shift from technology as an enhancement tool to technology as a transformative tool. This activity takes place on the transformative spectrum of the SAMR model, or the "deep end" of the SAMR Pool (see Figure 6.1). For more detail, visit my SAMR swimming lessons post on the HookED on Innovation website (http://mrhook.it/pool).

Following are some ideas for administrative uses of technology on the SAMR scale.

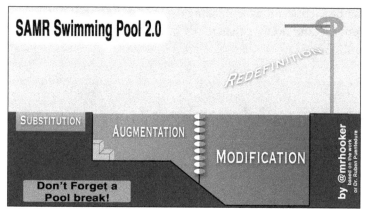

Figure 6.1 The SAMR swimming pool.

Substitution for Administrators

Substituting technology can be the most basic use of a device. Using a device for taking notes, reading articles and ebooks, or even giving an evaluation serve as examples. All of these activities can be done without technology; however, the very modeling of device use sends a powerful message.

Other examples include the use of the camera on a device or smartphone to take photos and capture evidence of learning and powerful moments throughout the school. This actually is close to augmentation, as you need technology to take a picture (unless you also work as a courtroom sketch artist on the side!). Again, this is basic use, but it is a powerful medium that's worth "a thousand words" and can be used with other tools to float even deeper into the SAMR pool.

Augmentation for Administrators

In Augmentation, technology is still an enhancement, but you are able to use the technology to accomplish tasks that would be more difficult or time-consuming without technology. I think of the walk-through example and how, in a substitutive use, you are simply typing notes that could also be handwritten. Now consider the possibilities if you were to enter those notes on some sort of Google form. When you hit submit, you would have all of your data instantly in a spreadsheet. Aggregate all the data from multiple walk-throughs and evaluations, and you'll start to see trends much more easily than you would without using technology.

Another example would be augmenting the substitutive task of taking photos and actually doing something with them digitally. You could share some of the best photos with parents and families in weekly newsletters, or, better yet, place the images on a computer screen and rotate the photos so parents can see them when they walk into your school.

Modification for Administrators

When I first started, administrators rarely moved past the augmentation phase when it came to their own use of technology integration. Modification refers to technology use that allows administrators to perform tasks that were previously not possible by any means.

Nowadays, with social media becoming more prevalent, I see more and more principals sharing their success stories via Twitter, Facebook, and even on blogs. While much of this is discussed in Chapter 9 (Reflection and Sharing), technology can move you into the modification and even the redefinition realm of SAMR when you start sharing your observations with the world.

This doesn't mean sharing actual teacher walk-throughs or official observations, but you could showcase a teacher's class or even a special school project or initiative by using social media. Take those same photos you used for both augmentation and substitution and share them with the community via Instagram or your school website. Save them and put them together for a culminating staff slide show that invites your staff and community to reflect on everything they have achieved during the previous year.

One other example I have to share happened recently at one of our elementary schools. A principal challenged his students to collect food for a canned food drive. It is not uncommon for schools to help raise awareness or collect food for food banks. The principal even said that if the entire school reached a certain goal, he'd dress up as the crazy character of the winning class's choice (a clown, a superhero, etc.). Needless to say, they hit their goal. And, rather than just sharing this moment with the winning class, he asked all of the students in the entire school to take out their iPads. Then he asked them to open up an app called Chirp (http://mrhook.it/chirp) and hold on for a special announcement. Chirp is an app that attaches messages, links, and even photos to an audio sound. So all a device needs is to be able to hear the little digital sound being sent from one speaker to a device's microphone to see what the message is. The principal then took to the school's announcement system and "chirped out" a picture of himself dressed up as a zany character. All 500 students in the school that had the Chirp app open received the photo on their device instantly!

TECH TIP

Find an old monitor or flat-screen TV that has some sort of VGA or HDMI input. You can find these for less than $150 for a 27-inch screen. Then, attach a device like an Apple TV ($69) or a Chromecast ($35) to the back of the TV. Either of these devices have a way of connecting a photo library from another machine or account that can be used as a screen saver and welcome screen to quickly showcase students and staff. Then, whenever you take photos on your professional device, it will automatically show.

Note: Be careful about mixing your personal photos into this collection, as it will auto update.

While this seems like a silly example of technology, it's a task that previously could not be done without technology, and his creative use of the schoolwide sound system was a powerful way of rethinking the messages he shared with staff and students.

Redefinition for Administrators

True redefinition of the classroom happens when students begin to come up with new ideas for completing tasks that were previously unimaginable. For an administrator, this can mean many things, but if you consider the students of the administrator being teachers in many cases, there are examples where principals have redefined learning from a leadership standpoint.

Take our original walk-through example and then get creative. Redefining the standard walk-through is as simple as recording a one-minute section of a lesson and then layering your own feedback into the lesson using an app such as Coach's Eye (http://mrhook.it/coach). Recording a brief segment of the lesson and then letting the teacher self-critique and point out areas of improvement not only helps them reflect, but it also gives them more owner-ship and self-direction in areas they need to improve. Suddenly, technology is allowing you to accomplish tasks you never thought possible.

Take that same concept and apply it to the photos you took around the school. Reflecting and sharing those same photos can be a transformative way of using technology to quickly share. Now take that concept a bit further and capture video snippets of students performing random acts of kindness. Continue to capture and share these videos, or take it to the next level and have students create their own song, script, and video vignette for it.

The "Lend a Hand" project at one of our local elementary campuses brings another example to mind. Although I share more about this story in the first book, the basis of the story is that two students were looking for ways to raise awareness about those who stand around and watch bullies and don't help the victim or attempt to stop the action. These students started the project by writing a poem together and by the end, had brought in some music (created by one of the student's uncles who happened to be in pop singer Kelly Clarkson's band) and then applied their own rap twist to it.

By the time it reached the desk of the campus principal, it was already becoming quite the phenomenon in fifth grade. The principal saw this and thought she had a couple of choices. One was to acknowledge that it was a good song and move on. The other was to acknowledge that it was a good song and make it into something bigger. By the time I got the phone call requesting my involvement, they were already planning to make a music video. Students had designed the tee shirts, the costumes, and even the vignettes. I had the pleasure of shooting the video, but since my footage was awful (it turns out that walking backwards, shooting video, and directing isn't something I can multitask), I decided to call on some high school film students who had actu-ally attended the very same elementary school several years earlier.

The final product was amazing to see, and the following year the school created the "Lend a Hand" program to combat bullying and also to celebrate students who exemplified good character traits. This isn't the type of project that happens every day, but a principal in charge of a school full of mobile devices will have opportunities like this arise from time to time. The job of the leader at that point is to put people in the right places to encourage redefinition on a grander scale. As you can see from Figure 6.2, this project even affected my daughter as she proudly wears her Lend a Hand tee shirt.

Figure 6.2 My daughter wearing the Lend a Hand tee shirt.

Expectations for Staff

Staff expertise and comfort level will vary in a mobile device initiative. Many will have been "successful" teachers in the traditional methods of teaching through the industrial age. A transformational shift in teaching and learning can be intimidating and disruptive to even the most even-tempered teacher.

Your job as a principal shouldn't be to come in like gangbusters and force teachers to change right away. Even if you followed some of the steps and advice in Chapter 5 on cultivating ownership, there will still likely be staff who are "just waiting until this trend goes away." In our high school, we faced a similar situation with a successful teacher who had received recognitions for AP scores in his class.

This teacher was extremely engaging and was really an effective teacher when it came to kids learning the content. But the introduction of mobile devices meant that his "tried and true" methods would need to be adapted or improved. He was initially reluctant, but setting expectations that staff don't have to change their entire teaching practice overnight can be helpful in getting teachers like this one on board.

Some of the biggest misconceptions among schools embarking on mobile device initiatives are that the technology will:

- Transform teaching and learning right away

- Make teachers unnecessary

- Cause the students to be "plugged in" 24/7

We will address the concerns of the third item later when we talk about the parent interaction piece. For now, let's focus on the first two misconceptions and how the setting of low expectations at first will get a larger majority of teachers to integrate technology, even if it's at the substitution level to start.

Early on, I did quite a bit of work with a principal who set her expectations for staff like this:

- Bring it to every meeting.

- Use it regularly.

She purposefully left the definition of "regularly" up to their judgment. She also didn't define what "use" really meant or what she was intending. However, teachers having their technology out, and using it even for basic functions, meant that they were part of the new norm. It also alleviated a lot of worry because teachers saw that they didn't have to remodel their teaching (at least not right away).

Expectations for Students

The campus principal is the place where the buck stops when it comes to discipline problems. Another major misconception in districts with mobile device initiatives is that the technology causes problems such as bullying and distraction. Although technology may increase the number of ways these things can happen, the root of the problem is still a human issue. In some ways, because technology is so traceable, it's easier to find bullies or students doing inappropriate things with their devices and online.

Because more and more of the necessary materials, textbooks, and learning management systems now exist on the devices, taking away devices should be a last resort. We've had a few instances where that has happened and the student (and teacher) make adjustments to life without technology. Since most teachers are still familiar with traditional education in terms of delivery structure, this isn't much of a stretch for them. However, as more and more states "go digital" with content, there will be fewer options for those relegated to using the hard copy version of materials.

One of our talented educational technologists (Lisa Johnson, @techchef4u) came up with an iPad Oath for all middle school students to sign (http://mrhook.it/oath). Students and parents viewed and agreed to this oath before receiving their device. The oath outlined expected behavior and possible consequences for inappropriate use.

Although the easiest solution (for both staff and parents) is to take the device away, we need to remember that besides the academic needs and uses of these devices, we are raising adults in our schools. At some point, they will need to self-monitor their behavior (presumably in college or career), so allowing them some room to do that is an important growth skill. We found that the second-offense consequence (the school emailing a screenshot to Mom and Dad) generally packed the most punch, and rarely did students go farther down that path.

Raising Expectations

Laying the groundwork with some low expectations for staff is good at an introductory level, but at some point, they need to swim deeper into the pool. This too can be done in phases by having teachers choose one or two lessons a semester that they would like to see rise up a notch on the SAMR scale.

Formative assessment tools can be some of the most quickly integrated and most effective when it comes to helping move the needle on student learning. Educational researcher John Hattie even lists formative assessment (when it is *for* learning, not just *of* learning) as a top-five indicator for student learning outcomes.

All this is to say that while you may have modeled the use of the device and set some minimum expectations, don't stop there. Although there are blanket expectations such as those I've mentioned in this chapter, you can also differentiate as a principal when it comes to different expectations for different staff. It wouldn't be effective to tell your high-tech staff members that he or she only has to take a device to meetings. Remember that there is always room for improvement. The ultimate goal is to have teachers look for ways to raise their own expectations and set goals that help to both integrate technology and provide meaningful ways to raise student learning outcomes.

CHAPTER 7

WALK-THROUGHS AND EVALUATIONS

n the early 2000s I was teaching first grade in a school in south Austin. My classroom was considered "high-tech" because I had four Compaq computers and a television, and I would sometimes hijack the one projector in the school so I could connect my laptop to it. Near the end of my first year teaching, I would have my first evaluation on a project around animals and their habitats.

I decided to take a risk and make the project one that would highlight the use of technology in my classroom. To set the tone, I created a three-minute movie of me doing my best Steve Irwin impersonation to get the students excited about the project. (Luckily, there was no YouTube back then.) The kids got excited, and I outlined what would happen over the next two weeks. There would be internet research, math problem integration, scientific data, some history, and of course language arts in the form of a poem written about their animal. It was project-based learning before that became a known entity in teaching.

I thought I nailed the lesson. The introduction video, the lessons using Clarisworks on the Compaqs, the internet research, and cross-curricular integration made this an intense project for 6-year-olds, but they all seemed very motivated to attempt it. However, when my evaluation came in, it was less than stellar. The assistant principal claimed in her write up that she didn't get why I was using technology with a lesson that all my peers were doing with construction paper and library books. She claimed the project was "way over the heads of the kids," and that I should stick with something simple because it was my first year teaching first grade (and, as it turned out, she used to be a first grade teacher, too).

This evaluation left me very frustrated and disappointed. At the same time it caused me to reflect on the activity itself and what learning was actually happening. In my efforts to make this amazing project, I focused too much on technology use rather than focusing on the skills being learned and demonstrated. I probably spent 90% of my energy and time to prepare the technology tools and the preview video. I lost focus on why I was doing the lesson in the first place. I think the concept had potential to be a powerful learning tool, but I needed to make sure the students were demonstrating what they learned rather than me telling them what to learn.

This situation is always in the back of my mind when observing teachers who are integrating technology in their classroom. When visiting classrooms in my district that really use 1:1 well, the technology is almost invisible. It's part of the classroom like the air in the room. Technology is a tool to enhance learning, but the learning isn't about the technology. In other words, lessons aren't focused on the device. A teacher wouldn't say "All right, kids, today we are going to do this app lesson on your iPads." That would be akin to me telling my first graders that their animal project was really about learning Clarisworks.

When done right, tech devices can help students own their learning. They will do their research, create presentations, and ultimately show they understand the concept. I once had the pleasure of observing a third grade teacher actually make the transition from "about the technology" to "about the learning" in front of my eyes.

This took place during a third grade lesson on the solar system. The teacher had done a lot of up-front work in understanding the technology and apps she would have the kids use. Kids worked in partners to develop a showcase for the celestial body they had been studying. The teacher told groups they had two tools they could use to display their final project: either Keynote or iMovie on their iPads.

Within minutes of going through the project, some students were starting to think about how they would demonstrate this. One student asked special permission to use an app called Explain Everything to present the findings of their planet. The teacher wasn't familiar with the app even though the students had it on their iPads for a few weeks. She wasn't comfortable letting them go off the path with something she wasn't familiar with, but then something magical happened.

She looked at me and then looked at her student and said, "Sure, but you'll need to explain how to use it with the class in case others want to use it, too." Within minutes, a couple of other students asked if they could use a different app to present their learning. She ended up limiting their number of options so as to not take away from the learning, but this left her with a stunned, yet pleased, look on her face.

Afterwards I asked her what she thought of the lesson and the things that happened with her students. She told me that she had taught that lesson for a few years and was just starting to figure out how to integrate technology into it, which is why she originally hesitated to allow additional technology. Having me in the room actually inspired her to take a risk, which gave me a lot of pride. It also made me wonder how I might build that capacity of risk-taking in teachers so that meaningful learning takes place with technology.

The answer lies with the campus administrator. I know many administrators do not feel very tech-savvy, nor do they know exactly what to look for in terms of technology when they are in a classroom. However, much like the teacher in my example, an administrator should be comfortable not knowing the technology because it's really all about the learning that's taking place in the classroom.

Classroom Observation

The remainder of this chapter is dedicated to the things administrators should look for when they walk into a classroom with technology. We will attempt to answer the following essential questions when observing technology use in learning:

- What are students doing?

- Who is leading the learning?

- Are students constructing their own learning?

- How are students reflecting and sharing their learning?

- How are you modeling all of this as a leader?

These five questions are useful when evaluating the extent to which learning is taking place in classes with or without technology; however, the questions are especially useful when observing tech-infused learning environments because technology tends to be the great amplifier when it comes to teaching and learning.

What Are Students Doing?

This may seem like an obvious question, but the answer isn't so simple. I remember when interactive whiteboards came out, and to be considered "proficient" with technology during an observation, a teacher basically had to touch the whiteboard. In a classroom where students have mobile devices, the learning has shifted from the wall to the students' hands.

Observing a classroom where all students have devices can be a bit overwhelming, but it doesn't have to be. Unlike observations of the past, where you would observe the teacher and his or her instruction, your focus now should be on the students. Are the students engaged? How are they using their devices? Are they using them to learn effectively?

As I mentioned in Chapter 2, simply using technology isn't necessarily a good thing. I once observed a lesson in a fourth grade class where the students were all engaged in a lesson on their iPads. I asked the teacher what the kids were doing with such enthusiasm and engagement. He told me he just digitized a math worksheet and gave it to them on their iPads to review using an annotation app. While this was very much an activity of "Substitution" on the SAMR scale, if student engagement was the only thing you were observing, you could say the students were using the technology effectively for that purpose.

When analyzing effective use of technology, don't limit it to student engagement. Sure, when it comes to learning, engagement makes learning not only possible, but plentiful. However, when evaluating effective use of the technology, the analysis should be much deeper and include answering some of the questions coming in the next few sections.

Who Is Leading the Learning?

If you've ever attended a traditional college classroom with auditorium seating, you know who is leading the learning. All the attention goes toward the front of the room. Never mind the concept of collaboration or student-centered learning in these lecture halls. The professor is the fountain of all knowledge.

Classrooms in K–12 education often look the same. Instead of hundreds of students in an auditorium, there are dozens of kids in a classroom full of desks in rows. Even with mobile technology, the learning and focus of attention is still on the front of the room. A quick look at the setup of the room can usually tell you who is leading the learning.

Observing a classroom that is effectively using mobile devices should have students who are leading the learning, not the teacher. Students actively engaged in the learning process, especially when working with mobile devices with access to the internet, means a lot less distraction and a lot more self-motivated learning. Classrooms that encourage this type of learning are often arranged in ways that are very different from the traditional "desks-in-rows" model. Students are mobile, involved in discussion, and researching information on the web.

Dr. Ruben Puentadura calls this shift from teacher-led to student-centered learning "transformational." In his SAMR model (Figure 7.1), there is usually a dotted line that represents this shift to transformation. In my SAMR swimming pool model, (http://mrhook.it/pool2), I equate transformation to that moment when you allow your kids to cross over to the deep end of the pool. You have to build their ability to swim before you throw them in the deep end, but once they are there, they can do so much more when it comes to technology integration.

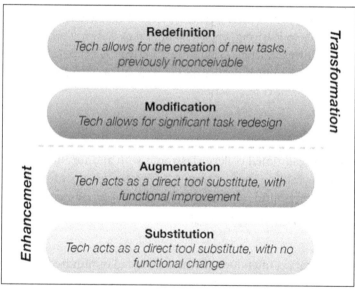

Figure 7.1 Ruben Puentadura's SAMR model.

Are Students Constructing Their Own Understanding?

When diving deeper into what students are doing with their devices, it is important to note how much time they spend consuming content versus creating it. One of the first obstacles we encountered with iPads was the presumption that they were primarily e-readers, gaming devices, and places to watch online videos. People viewed the iPads as consumption devices and "digital pacifiers" of sorts, because that's how they were largely used at home.

That assumption is wrongfully carried over to the classroom, but at times it's also perpetuated by how the devices are being used for learning. One of the first questions we got from teachers was whether their textbooks would be available on the devices. This is largely to be expected, because we've seen with Dr. Puentadura's SAMR model that users of technology first gravitate toward substitutive tasks. One of the other requests, largely from primary teachers, was to have certain "skill-building" app games put on the devices. Again, like textbooks, these apps fulfill certain roles in the classroom, but they are largely consumptive in nature.

The drawing "At School," by 19th-century French artist Jean-Marc Côté, actually depicts students plugged into their devices and absorbing content (Figure 7.2). This was his prediction for the classroom of 2000.

Figure 7.2 Côté's futuristic drawing titled "At School."

It's pretty remarkable how accurate his vision of the future was. A teacher shoves content into a machine that is pumped into the students' brains. Meanwhile, one poor student apparently misses out on learning because he is picked to turn a crank on a teaching machine. We could simply plug students into mobile devices and essentially have the same situation. In fact, much of instructional technology in the late 20th century and the early 21st century was meant to be mainly consumptive. Games such as Oregon Trail (https://en.wikipedia.org/wiki/Oregon_Trail) and Where in the World Is Carmen Sandiego? (http://tinyurl.com/npv8vd2) immersed students so deeply in the learning experience that they could play for hours without even knowing what was happening or that they were learning covertly. Although these games were a great way to introduce history and geography, they were consumptive in nature and content.

Aside from some simple choices and problem solving, there were never any opportunities for student creation or collaboration. While you can use digital tools and devices in the same fashion, it's a waste of money not to also use all the creative and collaborative options we now have because of increased access to the web.

When observing classrooms with mobile devices, the question in the back of your mind should be, how much creation is taking place? Are the students creating and constructing their own understanding?

How Are Students Reflecting and Sharing Their Learning?

"Education begins the gentleman, but reading, good company and reflection must finish him."
—John Locke (Ireland, 1884, p. 94)

Reflection is a powerful part of the learning process, yet it seems to be the first thing that goes when time is short in the content-driven classroom. Assessments end up doing double duty as reflection, but they are a poor substitute. Technology offers several opportunities for reflection, especially when all the students have their own devices.

Whether it be screen-recording something with a digital whiteboard app, writing a blog, video or audio recording themselves, or writing with pencil and paper and then snapping a picture, there are many ways to use devices to help with this process. When you are observing the mobile learning classroom, is reflection part of the process? If it isn't a regular tool in the classroom for learning, perhaps this would be a good time to reflect to yourself on why that is.

Another part of making learning more meaningful and impactful for kids is sharing what they learned. That sharing can happen with the teacher, with a peer, with a parent, with the whole class, or even online. One of the classic learning strategies is the learning pyramid (Figure 7.3). It shows the different ways that learning is retained. Participatory teaching through discussion and "by doing" shows significantly greater retention of learning.

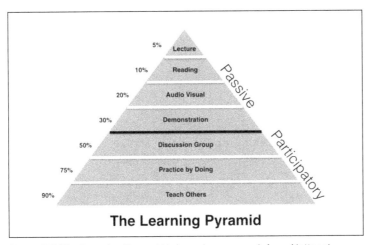

The Learning Pyramid

Figure 7.3 The Learning Pyramid is based on research from National Training Laboratories.

But the most powerful method of retention is by teaching others. Sharing your learning and explaining the process has a strong effect on that retention. Not all of that sharing process necessarily needs to happen in every observation (see reflection, earlier), but seeing examples of students sharing their learning throughout the classroom is a powerful way to leverage technology to check for understanding.

How Are You Modeling All of This as a Leader?

As I mentioned in Chapter 6 with the administrator version of the SAMR model, you need to be out in front in many ways, modeling all the things you hope to see in the classrooms when you do your walk-throughs and evaluations. Asking teachers to make the learning more student-driven and authentic should apply for all learners in your organization.

Think about opportunities where the staff plays the role of the student in your organization. That usually happens at faculty meetings and the occasional pre- and post-summative evaluation with the teacher. Those formats are tried and true in schools, but if you are trying to model the learning environment you want to see in classrooms, you shouldn't do it by having stand-and-deliver faculty meetings on a regular basis.

Meeting just because it's a date on the calendar and without a clear agenda are a couple of the reasons why meetings are bad. Check out David Grady's TED talk to discover more here: http://mrhook.it/meeting. When you think about all that you're trying to do with technology and the integration of technology in an authentic way, it begins to seem hypocritical to hold meetings based on the traditional rationale behind them.

Leaders have tried to replace meetings with mass email, which can be helpful to knock out messaging, but doesn't guarantee that everyone has read the message (see the "Tech Tip" on MailChimp for a way to check that). While, you could say the same thing about people sitting in a meeting and not listening, leveraging digital resources can help make the faculty meeting a much more enjoyable and meaningful event. However, this section isn't about knocking faculty meetings; it's about modeling and being an innovative leader in a mobile device initiative.

Some of the most innovative ways I've seen principals change the meeting structure is to actually "flip" the faculty meeting. In other words, share a video or record your message before the meeting to connect everyone to the same concept, then meet to get right to the task of problem-solving and collaborating. The great part about this is that you don't need to be a high-tech person to accomplish this. It can be as simple as recording your message on your phone and then sending it via email. With a little bit of extra effort, using a screen recording app or an animation app such as Tellagami (https://tellagami.com) can make those videos a little more creative and show-case different things the teachers can do in their own classes to flip or blend instruction a little.

Another idea that I've seen some principals employ is having a variety of staff lead parts of the meeting and even present a quick 5-minute summary about something they recently learned (either online or by attending a conference). This creates that flat leadership (mentioned in Chapter 1) and further cultivates the ownership of the staff (Chapter 6). By keeping these "mini-keynotes" to under 5 minutes, they help ease the nerves of a presenter who may not want to present in front of his/her peers, and it keeps the topics fresh and engagement up among the attending faculty. One way to take this concept and add a "digital twist" is to film these mini-sessions and create an online video catalog via YouTube or private Vimeo channel for staff to reference at a later date.

TECH TIP

Instead of sending out the standard mass email to share points, ideas, or ask for feedback, use Mailchimp (http://mailchimp.com) to create a drag-and-drop style newsletter that lets you see who's opened your emails and who's clicking on the links.

Regardless of how you plan to model and use the technology, always be aware of the fact that your staff, students, and communities are looking to you for leadership and paying attention to what you do or don't do. This doesn't mean you have to "fake it until you make it." You can use technology right away to carry out some basic tasks, such as taking attendance digitally or communication quickly, and by modeling in this way you send a message that the mobile device you use is here to stay and that you believe it.

CHAPTER 8

TYING IT ALL TOGETHER

Leading a mobile device initiative at the building level is a bit like cooking. It takes time, patience, and a good balance of ingredients and flavors to produce great soup. Adding ingredients without regard for how they blend can turn a tasty soup into leftover stew.

Each player in your initiative is an ingredient in the soup. Your job is to make sure you measure and weigh how much of a role each plays, not only with you but also with each other. If you have a group of teachers who are not on board with a certain concept or a technology department that doesn't support the things you want to change or implement, it could leave everyone with a bad taste in their mouths. The synergy of ingredients in your initiative will determine how successful it will be.

We've looked at things that campus leaders should avoid and discussed ways to cultivate shared ownership. We've seen how best to set positive expectations for staff and share with others. This chapter is dedicated to other key players and how interacting with them during your mobile device initiative will improve the flavor of your final product.

District Administration

The first book in this collection focused on district leaders and their role in a mobile learning initiative. They are the ultimate gatekeepers when it comes to approving ideas and discouraging others. Good district leaders work in harmony with campus leaders. One of the keys to this harmony is in the hands of campus leadership like you. Be certain to communicate early and often about any challenges your initiative may be facing and share the success you experience along the way.

As a district administrator, I can tell you that the days that I don't hear anything are the days that worry me the most. While some administrators crave those quiet times, it may mean that nothing is happening on campus. If the learning and teaching are not changing or adapting to the integration of technology, it means that the status quo is winning.

Real change and innovation comes hand in hand with disruption. Forgive my Yoda-like tangent here, but with disruption comes fear. With fear comes frustration. With frustration comes anger. With anger comes phone calls to the superintendent's office.

The mobile device initiative on your campus (and in your district) should have some agreed-upon goals and outcomes. These may not always be measurable in quantifiable data, but you should be able to share results toward those goals on a regular basis with district administration. The communication of progress, no matter how slight, will at least keep your administration in the loop and at best give you reasons to reflect regularly, reevaluate, adapt, and improve. As the principal, you have a lot of power and influence over the success or failure of a district initiative. You must be both a realist and a cheerleader for the change and improvement that comes with learning with mobile devices.

Teaching Staff and the Learning Environment

Getting to know your staff well and building trust with them are pivotal to improvement and use of technology in the classroom. Creating an environment that is both loose and tight allows for some autonomy while aligning certain expectations to a set of standards.

In my interview with Derrick Brown, he spoke about meeting teachers where they are and encouraging baby steps with them. For some, that may mean diving deeper and moving to the transformative side of the pool, but for others it could be something as simple as setting up their email. No matter what the change, as a leader you must support and celebrate those baby steps when it comes to using technology effectively.

As was mentioned in Chapters 6 and 7, you have to walk the talk with the expectation that teachers will follow suit. Do this in evaluations and faculty meetings, and leave the lines of communication open. By creating a web of communication and being a flat leader (Chapter 1), you've taken important steps toward getting that communication to happen on a regular basis with multiple leaders throughout your school.

Physical learning spaces are something I discuss in many of the other books in this collection, because it makes little sense to keep classrooms immobile when they have a mobile device initiative in place. Creating a collaborative learning space means a shift in the traditional "desks in rows" factory model of teaching. This can mean anything from beanbag chairs to fancy desks and tables on wheels. Regardless, conversations and strategies on how to use flexible furniture in optimal ways, along with a shift in pedagogy from teacher-led to student-centered models, can truly drive some transformative change and even cause hesitant teachers to rethink some of their methods.

Professional Learning

Modeling the effective use of technology during professional learning activities is important. You might not be the one leading the training each summer, but working ahead of time with those who do deliver professional learning is a great opportunity to go over your goals and objectives. This will help strengthen belief in your technology initiatives and increase buy-in.

Know that learning can come from a variety of resources, and that seat time doesn't always equate to learning time. One thing we have started doing in our district is giving professional learning credit for those participating in online Twitter chats. We had already given credit in the past for attending a webinar or taking an online course, so this was in some ways the next iteration of that. In fact, it was almost more intense in some ways, because the form they were required to fill out for proof detailed the things they learned and the things they were going to implement in their classroom. That's many times more meaningful and actionable than giving people a printed certificate or an online PDF for passing a class.

You want to create an environment where learning happens all the time, and where staff serve as the driving force behind what kind of learning they want to have. Although part of that comes from the mindset of the staff, as a principal you can exemplify the importance of learning by modeling yourself. Moderate that first Twitter chat with your staff, or stand up at the next faculty meeting and present your mini-keynote on something you just learned. Seeing a leader putting that to the forefront lets staff see the importance behind it and expresses your belief and buy-in about what you are trying to get everyone to learn.

Parents

The lines between home and school have been permanently blurred in some ways. With mobile devices and social media, connection is right at your fingertips and in your pocket. This ease of communication is also an opportunity for increased engagement with parents and your community.

Starting out with parent information nights is a good first step toward creating avenues of communication, but moving that interaction to the transformative level can have the most impact. Try bringing in a speaker to offer a different perspective, or creating an online course where parents can learn and interact with each other. As a reference, use your device to take a look at this public version of my last Digital Parenting 101 course: http://mrhook.it/101.

Having multiple modes of communication and many different people on your leadership team helps keep communication flowing between teacher, parent, and administrator. Using tools such as social media and MailChimp (see the Tech Tip in Chapter 7) are additional methods for engaging parents.

Google Hangouts (http://hangouts.google.com) is a great way to offer online office hours. These hangouts can host up to 10 people live and have an enabled chat room function so people who are not in the hangout can still post questions and ideas. What gives these even more impact is that you can choose to record (called Hangouts on Air), which auto-saves to your YouTube account. This is like taking the very static and impersonal FAQ page and putting your own twist and personality into it, all while modeling the use of technology to help collaborate and gather data.

Technology Department

Having spent nearly two years in a district technology department, I can tell you that getting a call or message from the principal can create a sense of urgency. As much as we want to take care of requests in the order we receive them, sometimes a call from a school leader allows them to jump to the top of the list. Add to that the fact that almost any change or request requires some level of extra work, and you can see why some technology support specialists become stressed when they see a principal's name on the caller ID.

With this in mind, state clearly to your IT department what you are trying to accomplish rather than asking for specific tools. Often, people in an IT department have a better idea or an optimized approach to what you are trying to accomplish. Also, for the purposes of relationship building, it's always a good idea to send some sort of kudos to members of the department who have helped you. IT staff are often unsung heroes. Much of the work they do goes on behind the scenes and without a lot of fanfare. Take time to recognize their hard work, and you'll find they are much more supportive of the ideas you have or requests you make.

Finally, it's important to have a member of the technology services department involved in some part of the early planning process of your mobile device initiative. They must be able to communicate what they can and can't control and understand which issues are technical (like a filter problem) and which issues are behavioral (like bullying). Because there can be a crossover between behavioral and technical issues in a 1:1 or BYOD program, maintaining open communication between campus administration and the technology department will fortify you against any challenges you may encounter. Knowing where the technology support stops and the administrative work begins is ultimately a conversation you will need to have between departments, but it's important to clearly define those at the onset of your initiative. Otherwise you might have a lot of conversations that start and/or end with "Oh, I thought you were taking care of that."

CHAPTER 9

REFLECTION AND SHARING

The world of education forces us to do more with less in a finite timeframe. This affects accountability, content, behavior, accommodations, diet, and the list goes on. As we strive to achieve our goals within these conditions, one of the first things to fly out the window is reflection. This situation is not exclusive to education. In the rat race that is modern life, we are constantly in motion and looking ahead. Rarely do we take a moment to see where we have been and how we got there.

Life as a principal of a mobile device initiative adds another layer of complexity and concern. You are part CEO, part financial manager, part instructional leader, and part psychiatrist. However, you should make it a part of your mission and routine to build in time for reflection and evaluate the path you have traveled. Depending on the goals of your initiative, it's important to think about the progress you've made and the distance you still need to travel.

How Deeply Is Your School Integrating Technology?

As I've mentioned in the SAMR Swimming Pool (http://mrhook.it/pool), there are times when technology will not be used, will be lightly used, or will be deeply integrated. The goal of technology use shouldn't be quantity of use—it should be quality of use. When we first introduced iPads, I could see teachers trying to use the technology in flashy ways. I remember visiting the classroom of a teacher who was using the iMovie Trailer feature. The kids were abuzz with discovery and excitement. When I asked the teacher what they were doing, she said, "Oh, they are just exploring the iMovie app."

Exploration and experimentation are an important part of any classroom. However, time is so precious in the modern classroom that harnessing the momentum of an "exploratory moment" to support a learning task can be powerful. Applying that learning momentum to an objective can take a "light" technology activity and make it much more meaningful.

A campus administrator who is evaluating technology use in the classroom must be able to see past any "cool" features of technology and see what the students are learning, what their process for learning is, and what kind of final product will demonstrate their learning. This can happen with or without technology, but the use of technology and mobile devices can amplify and enhance the learning experience.

This doesn't happen overnight. When educators introduced the pencil in classrooms around the country, teachers and students began exploring ways to use this modern tool instead of chalk. Eventually the pencil became an integrated part of the modern classroom. Lessons were not about exploring all the things you could do with a pencil; lessons focused on ways to use a pencil effectively for teaching and learning. Mobile device usage in the classroom is much the same.

Sharing Your Vision and Reflections

Sharing your vision and thoughts about what worked and what didn't is a pivotal part of good modeling. Capturing the reflections of parents, students, and teachers is important, but don't neglect your voice as campus leader.

Creating a blog may seem like a daunting task for a principal with a full plate; however, posting some short comments on social media or posting a few photos on Instagram that show what you've observed is a quick and easy way to communicate to all stakeholders. Showing others what learning looks like in this new mobile age will not only help you reflect, but also give your community a snapshot of the learning that is happening on your campus.

Tim Lauer (http://instagram.com/timlauer) is one of my favorite role models. Tim is the principal of Lewis Elementary in Oregon, and we had the pleasure of bringing him in to speak to our campus leaders about the importance of capturing the essence of learning and then sharing it on social media. Many of his community members as well as people from around the world follow his Instagram account. The combination of our smartphones, which essentially serve as mobile studios, and social media makes it easy for principals to do this.

TECH TIP

Use a tool like IFTTT.com to sync up your accounts. By "building a recipe" that links up your Instagram account and your school Facebook page, you can take a picture and auto-post it to both your Twitter account and your Facebook page with a single click.

As a direct result of Tim's visit, our district set a goal for all campus principals to have Facebook, Twitter, and Instagram accounts. While there are many other networks out there (Periscope being the new kid on the block), focusing on these three mainstream accounts allowed our campus leaders to send out a steady flow of information, reflection, and sharing in a variety of media. This is far more effective than relying solely on the typical email newsletter (which is likely to be read by just 50% of the people who receive it).

Use of these networks are growing among the 25-to-44 demographic, which also happens to be the majority of parents in current school districts. A look at a 2015 Pew study (http://mrhook.it/social) on frequency of use of social media sites also shows that Facebook and Instagram users actually engage with those accounts on an almost daily basis. Figure 9.1 shows the percentage of users who visit each site on a daily, weekly, or less frequent basis. As a campus leader, that's a powerful way to connect and tell the story of your school, and something that shouldn't be taken lightly.

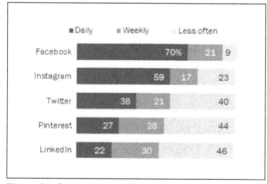

Figure 9.1 Daily social media check-ins (courtesy Pew Research Center, 2015).

What Adjustments Will Be Made in the Future?

You've launched your mobile device initiative and involved as many of the stakeholders as possible. You've avoided the things *not* to do and worked with all the groups involved to get some synergy and ownership around the initiative. You've had classroom observations and made sure teachers had access to effective professional learning. Now what do you do when it all doesn't take off as you expected?

The truth is, people (teachers) have a limited capacity to change their style or pedagogy. It can be done, but change needs to be incremental with constant checks for understanding, shared vision, and multiple opportunities for support. Not only do teachers have a limited capacity for change, but without clear goals and expectations, we've seen examples in Chapter 6 that highlight why this doesn't happen naturally.

Part of guiding this ship known as mobile learning is to check your course constantly and make corrections as needed. Many of those corrections are based on what you see in evaluations and walk-throughs. While that can be a good starting point, don't forget that you have a wealth of "customers" throughout your school who can point out things (via feedback) that need to be adjusted or supported.

Multiple modes of feedback can give you a variety of perspectives. Using technology to gather this data is not only a great way of modeling as a leader, it can also save you a ton of time.

The second part of that data gathering isn't so much technical (although you can make it such), but more about having critical and crucial conversations with your staff and students. That's right. Don't forget about the student in this process. In many ways they provide the most honest and authentic feedback.

Asking Students

I strongly encourage any campus leader to have daily conversations with students about how their learning is going. With so little time and so many commitments to other faculty, taking the time to check in with students regularly can fall by the wayside.

One of the benefits of having site visitors throughout the year is pulling together panels of students to hear their perspective on a mobile device initiative. We've hosted many of these throughout the year, and each time I hear the students' points of view, it greatly expands my hopes for the future of the program.

Once they get comfortable, students will tell you just about anything you care to ask. However, we do have policies about what students should share. For example, we ask that students never provide the names of specific teachers when they share stories about happenings in the classroom. Through these conversations, we have learned many useful things about class time. We discovered that teachers were using an app called Kahoot! (http://getkahoot.com) for formative assessment. We also learned about times when teachers were not as apt to allow students to take out their devices. It was through these conversations with students that we realized we had no uniform way of turning in digital assignments and that students needed a place to go for technology help and to recharge their devices.

With the exception of a "free game day," we've taken students' suggestions to heart and tried to use their feedback as means for improvement. When our library was making a transformation into a research center, our district librarian and master design thinker, Carolyn Foote (http://twitter.com/technolibrary), thought it might be a good idea to engage students with part of the redesign.

One area that had seemingly gone unused with the proliferation of mobile devices was the research section of the library. The majority of these shelves housed old research textbooks and encyclopedias—all information that students could easily access on their phones or new devices. With a limited amount of plugs on the wall and bookshelves that covered the outside windows, it was decided that this would be the perfect section to put some student suggestions into motion.

And so, with guidance from students, direction from our librarian and architect, and inventiveness of our maintenance department, the "Juice Bar" was born (Figure 9.2). This space features a location for students to get technology assistance, to collaborate on a project, and to charge their devices (we added plugs around the windows with USB connectors). The students even came up with the name, presumably based on the concept of your device needing some juice to recharge. Although this is a big example, it shows the power of reflecting on your initiative and asking your key customers for feedback to make the experience better.

Figure 9.2 Our library's "Juice Bar" is a place where students can get assistance with technology, collaborate, and charge their devices.

Having an Open Dialogue with Parents

Although it can sometimes be difficult to deal with parents—especially those who seem irrational—it is essential for campus leaders to seek out opportunities to involve them. One such opportunity arose in the middle of our second year of implementation. There was a tremendous amount of disagreement among our community of parents around how much digital responsibility the students should have on their devices. Many parents were dealing with the challenge of having to juggle schoolwork, screen time, smartphones, and distraction at home with technology. Now they would have to adjust to the fact that their child's homework was on a device that they didn't understand.

With the support of campus principals, we called in a variety of parents to have a panel (much like the student panels mentioned in the section above) to gather feedback and have a conversation about the challenges of the new digital realm (Figure 9.3).

Figure 9.3 Parent panels allowed us to have conversations about issues that didn't occur to us.

This panel not only provided the campus with feedback, it also took some of the pressure off the local administration. By showcasing people within the community as experts who could deal with a variety of problems and solutions, we built the capacity of the community and made them realize that one person is not the fountain of all knowledge. Capturing all of this on a livestream made it even more successful because it meant that hundreds of more parents could watch the event later and still feel that they were a part of the conversation (livestream recording available here: http://mrhook.it/panel).

Using Surveys as Reflection and Growth

Sending out surveys for feedback isn't an exact science. Sending something out too early won't result in authentic feedback. Sending a survey with hundreds of questions won't get anyone to answer. However, sending out timely surveys with information that you actually revisit and put into action can be one of the fastest and easiest ways to crowdsource data from a variety of places.

Each survey should focus on different components of your initiative. Parent surveys are some of the best ways to get honest feedback about how a mobile device initiative affects home and school life. Student surveys can help you understand how the devices are being used in class. A survey for teachers could give your staff a chance to talk about their fears and list things they want to learn. Use these surveys to gather information about the initiative and to get ideas for growth and support.

Professional Learning

The idea behind reflecting and sharing really comes into play when talking about professional learning. Do you make it a point to provide time for reflection with your group? Do you encourage avenues to share what you learned? Are you building in times for reflection throughout your professional learning at different points of your initiative?

Time to reflect is often the first thing to go when it comes to teacher training, but providing time for reflection throughout the year can be especially valuable. Encourage staff to share their reflections with you as part of a summative evaluation process. By reviewing the variety of ways in which they have implemented technology, you can make adjustments to what they are learning professionally and see where they might need more support.

Support

Part of the reflection and evaluation process involves your looking for ways to improve your program. Sometimes those improvements can be logistical. Perhaps there's a new way to provision apps (that's what happened to us) or maybe there is a better way to monitor what students are doing online. Having that open line of communication with the technology services department (refer to Chapter 8) means looking at how to best use their support.

Our model before the 1:1 mobile device initiative was to distribute all iPads to English classes throughout the high school. Our thinking was that we could hand out devices and then give a brief orientation about best practices to each student. While this made sense to us, the approach spread our technology support staff pretty thin. The next year, following a group reflection of the rollout, we decided to stage the distribution centrally, which helped us leverage fewer staff. We then recorded the device orientation as a video for each student to watch in class rather than place presenters in each classroom.

If we didn't build in that time for reflection during the distribution process, our support for the initiative wouldn't have been able to improve. As the leader of this initiative, you need to be looking for ways to optimize the process at all times. Even if you don't understand the technical side of things, it's a good idea to ask if things can be done better.

Dreams and Hopes

Every leader of an initiative should take a moment to lay out his or her dreams and hopes for the program. Whether it be improving student engagement or increasing reading scores, having these goals written down will help keep you on the path should things start to go astray. Although it's not necessary to share these with the world, sharing them with your staff will help them stay focused on the mission at hand.

There will always be variables beyond your control when leading a campus on a mobile learning initiative. The internet will go down when you least expect it. Online textbooks will crash and fail to load as promised. Parents will storm your door for "traditional" learning materials because of technical issues they had or because they saw a TV program that pronounced technology to be bad for kids. Teachers will get frustrated, and some may take years to buy in.

Despite these mini-tragedies, there will be an even greater number of successes. You'll get to see students do things never before imaginable. You'll see a teacher with 37 years of experience become reinvigorated with the new ways she can reach her students. You'll hear from parents about how their child is now more excited to go to school or how they are able to stay more organized because of digital materials.

No matter what the reason or story, know that this will be the most challenging but also the most rewarding initiative you will ever be a part of.

ISTE STANDARDS

The ISTE Standards for Administrators (ISTE Standards·A)

All school administrators should be prepared to meet the following standards and performance indicators.

1. **Visionary Leadership**

    Administrators inspire and lead development and implementation of a shared vision for comprehensive integration of technology to promote excellence and support transformation throughout the organization. Administrators:

    a. Inspire and facilitate among all stakeholders a shared vision of purposeful change that maximizes use of digital age resources to meet and exceed learning goals, support effective instructional practice and maximize performance of district and school leaders.

    b. Engage in an ongoing process to develop, implement and communicate technology-infused strategic plans aligned with a shared vision.

    c. Advocate on local, state and national levels for policies, programs and funding to support implementation of a technology-infused vision and strategic plan.

2. Digital Age Learning Culture

Administrators create, promote and sustain a dynamic, digital age learning culture that provides a rigorous, relevant and engaging education for all students. Administrators:

a. Ensure instructional innovation focused on continuous improvement of digital age learning.

b. Model and promote the frequent and effective use of technology for learning.

c. Provide learner-centered environments equipped with technology and learning resources to meet the individual, diverse needs of all learners.

d. Ensure effective practice in the study of technology and its infusion across the curriculum.

e. Promote and participate in local, national and global learning communities that stimulate innovation, creativity and digital age collaboration.

3. Excellence in Professional Practice

Administrators promote an environment of professional learning and innovation that empowers educators to enhance student learning through the infusion of contemporary technologies and digital resources. Administrators:

a. Allocate time, resources and access to ensure ongoing professional growth in technology fluency and integration.

b. Facilitate and participate in learning communities that stimulate, nurture and support administrators, faculty and staff in the study and use of technology.

c. Promote and model effective communication and collaboration among stakeholders using digital age tools.

d. Stay abreast of educational research and emerging trends regarding effective use of technology and encourage evaluation of new technologies for their potential to improve student learning.

4. Systemic Improvement

Administrators provide digital age leadership and management to continuously improve the organization through the effective use of information and technology resources. Administrators:

a. Lead purposeful change to maximize the achievement of learning goals through the appropriate use of technology and media-rich resources.

b. Collaborate to establish metrics, collect and analyze data, interpret results and share findings to improve staff performance and student learning.

c. Recruit and retain highly competent personnel who use technology creatively and proficiently to advance academic and operational goals.

d. Establish and leverage strategic partnerships to support systemic improvement.

e. Establish and maintain a robust infrastructure for technology including integrated, interoperable technology systems to support management, operations, teaching and learning.

5. Digital Citizenship

Administrators model and facilitate understanding of social, ethical and legal issues and responsibilities related to an evolving digital culture. Administrators:

a. Ensure equitable access to appropriate digital tools and resources to meet the needs of all learners.

b. Promote, model and establish policies for safe, legal and ethical use of digital information and technology.

c. Promote and model responsible social interactions related to the use of technology and information.

d. Model and facilitate the development of a shared cultural understanding and involvement in global issues through the use of contemporary communication and collaboration tools.

© 2012 International Society for Technology in Education (ISTE), iste.org. All rights reserved.

REFERENCES

Friedman, T. (2014). *How to get a job at Google.* Retrieved from www.nytimes.com/2014/02/23/opinion/sunday/friedman-how-to-get-a-job-at-google.html?hp&rref=opinion&_r=1

Ireland, A. (1884). *The book-lover's enchiridion.* London: Simpkin, Marshall & Co.

Johnson, L. (2013). *The iPad oath: 10 rules for iPad use in the classroom.* Retrieved from www.teachthought.com/the-future-of-learning/technology/the-ipad-oath-10-rules-for-ipad-use-in-the-classroom

Lovecraft, H. P. (1927). Supernatural horror in literature. *The Recluse, 1,* 23–59.

Pew Research Center (2015). *The demographics of social media users.* Retrieved from www.pewinternet.org/2015/08/19/the-demographics-of-social-media-users

Puentadura, R. (n.d.). *SAMR: Methods for transforming the classroom.* Retrieved from http://www.hippasus.com/rrpweblog/archives/2013/10/25/SAMR_MethodsForTransformingTheClassroom.pdf

9 781564 843746